You Are #1

The Science and Reasons Behind Why We Remember Some of Our Teachers, Forever

Dr. Holly Blair

Dr. Rick Jetter

Copyright © 2022 by Holly Blair & Rick Jetter
Published by EduMatch®
PO Box 150324, Alexandria, VA 22315
www.edumatchpublishing.com

All rights reserved. No portion of this book may be reproduced in any form without permission from the publisher, except as permitted by U.S. copyright law. For permissions contact sarah@edumatch.org.

The names and identifying details of certain individuals have been changed to protect their privacy.

These books are available at special discounts when purchased in quantities of 10 or more for use as premiums, promotions fundraising, and educational use. For inquiries and details, contact the publisher: sarah@edumatch.org.

ISBN: 978-1-953852-69-4

"Dancing fires on the beach . . .
singing songs together . . .
though it's just a memory . . .
some memories last forever."

--From the song, "Lakeside Park," by RUSH

Dedication

In honor of the countless numbers of incredible teachers who are the "dancing fires" in the memories of everyone on this planet.

YOU ARE #1 in our book!

Contents

Introduction	xi
1. How Neuroscience Explains Your Good and Bad Teacher Memories	1
2. Because Teachers Care	11
3. Because Teachers are Nice	21
4. Because Teachers Are Funny	35
5. Because Teachers are Exciting	49
6. Because Teachers are Involved	61
7. Because Teachers Understand	77
8. Because Teachers have Wisdom	87
9. Because Teachers are Human	99
10. Because Teachers are Devoted to the Profession	109
Conclusion	123
Appendices	129
References	171
About the Authors	177
Bring "You Are #1" to Your School or Organization	179

"I spent all my time at school in the library. Bad teachers can teach you to learn on your own."

GREGORY COLBERT

Introduction

The Smelly Breath and Laziness of Mr. Michaels

No one liked Mr. Michaels. He was a terrible teacher on top of having poor hygiene and smelly breath. *Yet, he will be remembered, forever, by his students, somehow.*

Mr. Michaels taught 9th Grade English in Los Angeles, California, for thirty-five years before retiring. He smoked about two packs of cigarettes each day. Some students thought that he also had a bottle of rum in his desk. He passed out grammar worksheets and sat on an old, squeaky wooden desk chair that spun around from side to side so he wouldn't have to get up. Students would have to come up to him when they finished their worksheets and get the "red pen treatment" to either move on to a new worksheet or report back to their desks to correct their terrible mistakes.

Some students would never get up from their desks even if they finished diagramming their sentences because of Mr. Michaels' bad breath. It was reported from multiple students that the "smell" came from Mr. Michaels' rotten teeth, cigarette odor, and olive-loaf-luncheon-meat-filled breath. Kids saw the sandwiches sitting on his desk. A bag of corn chips was usually next to his sandwiches because Mr. Michaels liked to put the corn chips on his sandwiches in order for something to feel crunchy between his old, disgusting rotten teeth.

Former students could still hear him crunching when they reported this story to us.

Usually, there were two sandwiches and two bags of chips--one stinky meal for the morning and one for the afternoon. A fresh box of Marlboros could be seen poking out of Mr. Michaels' front shirt pocket. He also had a cough that accompanied his deep chuckle when he mocked students for their incorrect worksheet answers.

Mr. Michaels deserves kindness and we are not reporting this story to you in order to bash him. That's no way to start off a book that *celebrates* teachers. Instead, what **YOU ARE #1** does is to celebrate the teaching profession by sharing stories (both good and bad) while merging it with the neuroscience behind the role that our memories play in remembering our teachers, forever. Teachers have incredible impacts on our lives and teachers can be #1 in only *two* regards:

1. They can be #1 in our memories in a *positive* way.
2. They can be #1 in our memories in a *negative* way.
3. We guess there is a #3, but it is invisible, really, when we don't remember *anything* about our teachers, whatsoever!

There are loads of teachers who have neither positive or negative impacts on our memories. They are either easily forgotten or are just lumped into the "OK" category. They were just "there" in our lives without much significance, either way.

Teachers have incredible influence over how they will be remembered - in either a positive or negative manner. Will teachers be championed or mocked? Will they be mentioned as the *reasons* why their students go on to become teachers or enter into a profession or trade because of a teacher?

We all have stories about our favorite teachers of all time and not-so-favorite teachers of all time. Why do we, sometimes, remember our teachers more than our doctors, pastors, or even extended family members or other relatives? Easy: Teachers are with students for long periods of time and arrive in our lives when experiences are constructed with enormous impacts on our pre-adolescent brains. In other words, **teachers help to construct our childhoods.**

We have gathered information from hundreds of people, including lots and lots of educators, that we want to share with you in this book. A Google Survey was sent out through social media channels (Twitter, Facebook, and LinkedIn) for collecting immediate responses and narratives from anyone within the profession of education (or even those outside the profession) who wanted to share with us. Over 500 respondents filed their responses on our survey and dozens and dozens of respondents shared actual narrative comments with us which you will find in the appendices of this book. Out of the pool of respondents, approximately half were teachers, some were school leaders, and the other half included parents and even students as young as age nine. Almost all fifty states were represented in our research and diversity and gender patterns of participation were included so our research pool was not lopsided.

We learned that 86% of our survey respondents remembered negative teachers and 99% of our survey respondents remembered their positive teachers. While we aim to decrease the negative number, obviously, what is interesting to learn is that both of these percentages are super, super high! If a president of the United States of America had an approval rating of 86% or 99%, that would be incredibly *historical*, wouldn't it?

So, strap on your seatbelt as we share with you some powerful stories about others' childhood experiences and memories of their teachers.

But, before we get to that, let's learn just how the human brain preserves our positive and negative experiences in ways that we cannot possibly imagine. That is, in what ways can neuroscience provide powerful information about how our memories are activated by our positive and negative thoughts of teachers' actions and behaviors?

INTRODUCTORY BOOK STUDY CHALLENGE

---

1. Write a list of your most memorable teachers (good and bad).
2. Write down WHY you categorize them as good or bad.
3. Try not to think of EVERY teacher that you've had, only the ones that jump out at you right away as you remember your teachers, overall.
4. Analyze: What do the good ones have in common?
5. Analyze: What do the terrible ones have in common?
6. Reflect: How do YOU want to be remembered by your students?

"You are a data-collecting-being and your memory is where your life has lived."

KEVIN HORSLEY

Chapter 1

How Neuroscience Explains Your Good and Bad Teacher Memories

We find it incredibly interesting that our research asked a central question about the level of schooling that memories have been generated for people over time. Check this out:

Our question was: "At what level of schooling did you have the MOST positive memories of your teachers?" Look at the response percentages:

42% = Elementary School
11.5% = Middle School
42% = High School
4.5% = Post Secondary School

What is most noticeable to us is that memories from high school were EQUAL to memories of elementary school which is even *further* back in our lives--YEARS earlier, in fact, which solidifies the memories even longer! This holds true for a similar question about negative experiences: "At what level of schooling did you have the most negative memories of your teachers?" Look at the response percentages:

31% = Elementary School
21.4% = Middle School
39% = High School
8.6% = Post Secondary School

Again, going back to elementary school tells us that memories can be forever forged in our minds. Maybe a bit more analysis after the stats.

Let's briefly revisit the story about Mr. Michaels for a moment. If you think about how this story was portrayed, specific *senses* were described as part of the memory recall process and those senses triggered emotions at some point. The sense of smell captured "rotten teeth," "cigarettes," and "olive loaf." "Laziness" was represented through Mr. Michaels' squeaky chair while the "crunching" of corn chips on his sandwiches made students' stomachs turn because the sense of sound was reactivated for his students as they remember Mr. Michaels as an unpleasant teacher.

We won't belabor presenting to you some research about how memories of our teachers become so strong over time that they become solidified in our memory center. Brief and to the point, let us examine a quick summary so you can see how this all works.

The Neuroscience of Memory

Our sensory capacities assist us to tell stories from the past. They are activation points that the brain stores into its compartmentalized cache. Sensory components trigger and evoke emotions and those emotions lead us to remember something as either good or bad, pleasant or unpleasant, or even happy or sad.

Here's how it works, according to neuroscientists: The amygdala is the center for emotions in the brain where neurons assign good or bad feelings (known as "valence") to some sort of human event or encounter. The inner workings of valence by focusing on one particular section of the amygdala, called the basolateral amygdala, can help us to understand how memory is triggered through emotions because emotions are triggered through our senses. By looking at these interactions and system structures close up, there are distinct and diverse "neighborhoods," in which valence is determined through connections to other regions in the brain and interactions with the basolateral amygdala itself (Gohd, 2020).

When these things come together, we are left with deep, meaningful memories that explain why so many people remember a favorite teacher or their worst-nightmare-of-a-teacher! According to Trafton (2015),

> Everyone knows that we can learn about both positive and negative experiences, but it has never been shown how one structure can contribute to encoding two diametrically opposed emotional outcomes. Each cell projects and determines whether it encodes a positive or a negative memory in the brain. Think of it like a deli counter refrigerated case where all the meats are stored into their own slots. We all have this brain function as part of our daily, typical functioning just like how our heart beats involuntarily and memory is strengthened through our exact episodic events including the actors and actresses on the stage of the teaching profession. There are some good actors and there are some terrible ones (and we can tell high quality from low quality performances).

Therefore, recalling old memories can have a cinematic quality (either good or bad). Humans remember life events through a series of associations--emotionally charged and sensory-laden. When retrieving an old memory, neocortical activity occurs in areas linked to all the separate elements that create the memory in the brain. The degree to which someone can vividly remember a past memory correlates directly with the level of hippocampal activity.

The hippocampus connects various neocortical regions and brings them together into a holistic and cohesive "event engram" or neural network that represents a specific life event of memory from the past (Trafton, 2015). This is the essence of memory activation (and reactivation) over time, and teachers have an incredible impact on what we remember because we will store it in our brain as either positive or negative. Remember, the hippocampus is a complex brain structure embedded deep in the temporal lobe of the brain. It is found smack, dab in the center of the brain in fact, and is vital to our memories. Feels a bit brief, but it may be me.

The Continuum of Positive and Negative Memories

So, how should we classify a positive or negative memory and what does it really mean in *You Are #1*?

Let's think about the negative characteristics of teachers. Most of it is common sense. When you see how we stumbled across the positive characteristics of teachers for the chapters in this book, those, too, are common sense, but it is interesting for us to see how our survey respondents classified their greatest positive memories of the teachers they had in the past and why they remember them, forever!

Here are some typical nightmarish characteristics of teachers that we could probably all agree on for how we would set up the classification of our negative memory-deli-counters:

1. Corporal punishment
2. Bullying (to also include any of the specific behaviors below, physically, mentally, or emotionally)
3. Threatening
4. Shouting (including berating)
5. Belittling

6. Humiliating
7. Scapegoating
8. Rejecting
9. Isolating
10. Ignoring

These would be the typical categories of negative experiences as they relate to thinking about and remembering a teacher in a negative fashion. We believe that if we conducted our research to include both positive and negative memories of our teachers that one or more of these negative categories would be in common with anyone whom we asked about regarding a terrible teacher that they remember.

Mr. Michaels, for instance, would fall into the categories of "rejecting," "isolating," or even "ignoring." The smelly breath and gross lunch items only enhance the memories of students' negative experiences through the lens of sensory agility and emotional responses to something unpleasant, thus making the experience a negative one overall, and possibly lasting for a lifetime.

What we love the most about *You Are #1* is that the hundreds and hundreds of survey respondents who wrote to us about the positive memories that they hold when thinking about the most memorable teachers they have had are attributes divided into nine essential categories of positive memories. The following nine areas are the central focus of each of our remaining chapters as we celebrate teachers by sharing with you what others said about their teachers who fit into one or more of these positive categories and for these reasons are the teachers whom we remember, forever. The positive reasons why we remember our teachers are because they are:

1. Caring
2. Nice
3. Funny
4. Exciting

5. Involved
6. Understanding (which is different from "caring")
7. Wise
8. Humanistic (has been through pain, struggle, or hurt before)
9. Devoted (to the teaching profession)

If you are an educator who has picked up this book, thank you for relating yourself with one or more of these nine core areas of distinction. If you are not an educator, we cannot wait for you to read the stories that paint the canvas of the teaching profession by which you may recall one of your finest teachers of all time!

So, let's begin to celebrate teachers, together, and not wait for another page of cigarettes and olive loaf!

CHAPTER 1
BOOK STUDY
CHALLENGE

1. What are some sensory characteristics that you remember about your (good and bad) teachers from the past?

2. What types of feelings do those sensory characteristics have for you as you remember your teachers?

3. What are some sensory characteristics that you think your students, or others, will remember you by, forever?

4. List as many pleasant sensor-triggering things that you can about yourself.

"Nobody cares how much you know until they know how much you care."

THEODORE ROOSEVELT

Chapter 2

Because Teachers Care

Caring teachers were important to our survey respondents with an approval rating of 80.3%.

Mrs. Smith was one the greatest teachers of all time. She was a fifth grade teacher and she taught her students how to love learning math and science and she read the coolest books to the class that the world has ever experienced. She knew every student, their families, and greeted them each day with a warm hello because they truly believed that just their presence in her class made her day even better. They looked forward to going to school each and every day just to see what exciting things she would bring to the class that was going to make them better people.

She was the primary reason many became teachers. To this day, decades after entering the profession, they look up to her as a premiere educator. To them, Mrs. Smith is the epitome of what a phenomenal teacher should be. They remember almost everything about her: personality, sense of humor, and making learning fun, and they knew she truly cared about them and their education.

Don't get us wrong, our educational experience (pre-kindergarten through doctoral) is filled with more good teachers than bad ones. We can remember most of their names but when thinking about it, other than the grades or subjects they taught, we really cannot say what we learned or why we thought they were "good." Maybe it's because they weren't "bad" teachers? We're talking about the *really* bad teachers-- you know, the ones that make you realize that, even though, at the beginning of your teaching career, you did not know what you were doing, but you did, however, know exactly what **NOT** to do.

Look at how Mr. Jones is a complete nightmare of a teacher:

Mr. Jones once called a girl up to the front of the class and publicly announced that not only did he not like her, but that his family did not like her because he told them how horrible she acted in his class. (This is only because he sat her in the second to the last row, only to have a bully who sat behind her literally poking her, pulling her hair, and telling her how much of a loser she was for the first quarter of school). She finally had enough and started standing up for herself because when she told Mr. Jones, he did nothing. It was the only class that her parents allowed her to drop because she was beyond miserable. She spent more time in the principal's office that first quarter of her school year than she did the rest of her school life! (Please note: she became a principal and has been for over 15 years!).

We have all had a Mrs. Smith or a Mr. Jones in our educational experience. Throughout this book, there are vignettes from hundreds of people from all over the world stating their recollections of their most memorable teachers--both the #1 favorite and the #1 worst.

When asked to name who their favorite or worst teacher was, people do not have a difficult time remembering them. Why is that? Why is it that some stand out more than others? Maybe it's because teachers either truly care about students or they care about other things and teaching simply becomes an after-thought for them--forgetting the importance of childhood and making connections. The same could be said for other professions.

According to a Watson Caring Science Institute study (2021) that examined the personality of nurses, a major conclusion of the study was:

> The dynamic of transpersonal caring (healing) within a caring moment is manifested in a field of consciousness and intentionality. The transpersonal dimensions of a caring moment are affected by the nurse's consciousness and heart centered presence in the caring moment, which in turn affects the field of the whole.

While the Institute is focused on the nursing profession, the same rules apply in education. If the teacher truly cares for the students, then transpersonal caring takes place and the students are positively affected. This is not a "fake it 'til you make it" scenario. Teachers either care about the well-being and education of their students or they do not.

If you are an educator, what type of educator are you? Are you a mediocre one for whom people may remember your name and what you taught with few details as to what you were like? Are you one who rocks the world of the majority of your students and they remember for the rest of their days just how spectacular, fun, engaging, and caring you were for the one outstanding year you were with them? Or are you the one that when they think back on their educational experience, they think, "The world really could have used more oxygen," every time they spoke?

Let us pose this question for you: What did you have for lunch three days ago? It is not a loaded question. We are going to guess that before you knew the answer to that question, you had to think, "What day is today?" and then count back to what the day was three days ago. Then you had to try to stretch your memory to remember what you had for lunch. For the record, most people struggle with this answer. Why? Unless you had a spectacularly great or horrific meal or unless something exceptional happened while you were eating that meal, your brain did not release the higher level of hormones needed to create a memory in your frontal lobe.

According to Sprenger (2020),

> The frontal lobe houses the structures where most brain activity occurs when people care about each other, trust each other, and want to be friends. The limbic system houses the amygdala, the seat of emotion. The limbic system is loaded with receptors for chemicals for two different hormonal systems: the stress-response system and the trust/love system. When we are stressed, cortisol is released, triggering the stress response. By contrast, when we care about and trust someone, oxytocin is released, and we feel connected.

It's incredible to think about the impact that teachers have over every student they come in contact with simply by caring about them.

Read further the following story related to these findings:

> When I was an elementary student, I was diagnosed with a processing disability. I did know why but subjects like math and reading just never made sense. I thought I was dumb because no matter how hard I tried, I felt like I just could not do it. Through the determination and support of an elementary school teacher who never gave up on me, I slowly developed the skills to not only succeed in the subjects, but excel. Mr. Red always showed that he cared. He offered sound feedback and advice, never dwelled on our sometimes naughty behaviors. He knew the personal backgrounds of each of his students. He was "that teacher" which everyone loved and respected.

When remembering Mr. Red and the positive impact he had on this person, oxytocin was released making the feeling as real as the time when they were in his class. It is easy to imagine the smile as they recounted the memory and a feeling of happiness flooded throughout their body. Mr. Red cared about this person to the point where they were not going to give up on themselves.

Now, read this passage in the converse:

> After two weeks of kindergarten, I was moved to a first grade class. It was a Friday, and it was time for a spelling test. Ms. Black slapped a piece of paper down on the desk and said, "If you're so smart, you can take the spelling test." I remember crying and failing the spelling test. I do not remember anything else about first grade.

By contrast, when remembering this first grade teacher, cortisol was once again released and the body's stress-response system was kicked into high gear. This memory alone creates the body's stress-response system to relive that experience and actually block the rest of the year:

> In this dysregulated mode, the brain orders the release of adrenaline and cortisol that aid in the short-term behaviors that result in safety-seeking and survival. The psychologist Daniel Siegel refers to this as being in our 'downstairs brain' – and in the school setting this part of our brain ejects us from the learning mode, rendering us unable to teach or learn (Souers & Hall, 2020).

In both scenarios, Mr. Red and Ms. Black trigger the limbic system and create the hormonal connection for people with these memories and then store sensory memories in the frontal lobe of the brain. These were memories from decades ago, yet when asked to recall them, the memories and feelings from those experiences flood the brain.

Your lunch from three days ago most likely did not cause your body to create enough oxytocin to forge a life-long memory, nor did the experience create enough adrenaline and cortisol to scar you for life!

So, "caring" is defined by our research respondents in the following three ways:

1. Teachers who "care" wake up in the morning and give a damn (about you and about your achievement). They strive to plan for success.
2. Teachers who "care" are devoted to doing good things each day. They are sad when things go wrong and feel guilty when they inadvertently do something that does not help students.
3. Teachers who "care" do not settle for mediocre. They do not want to be the sandwich that is easily forgotten.

We started with this characteristic, not only because it was THE most widely cited characteristic of powerful teachers, but because "caring" is a prerequisite for good teaching and good teachers. Teachers have to care about something and that something should be students, first, above course content or subject matter. Memorable teachers care about their students, but even more powerful, we remember someone because they cared about us--students who are assigned to a teacher and that teacher can either make us, break us, or do little to influence us either way.

Throughout this book, you will read stories from real people with fond and not so fond memories about their educational experiences. These stories are going to be backed by the science we presented and research that we cross referenced our study with, and you will see just how these experiences affect the development of the human brain. You are going to be challenged to rethink what type of educator you are and the one you want to be. You will be asked to reflect and question what you can do to become the "rockstar" memorable teacher that you know you want to become. Why?

Because YOU are #1!

CHAPTER 2
BOOK STUDY CHALLENGE

Take a few minutes and reflect on who you are as an educator. As of today, how do you think your students will remember you as a teacher?

1. Then list at least one thing that you KNOW that your students will remember about you: positive or negative.
2. Go beyond the sensory activity from the last chapter and now get to the actions that define you as a person and teacher.
3. What actions define you as a good teacher?
4. What regrets do you have that made you feel like a terrible teacher? How did you fix those actions or habits?
5. What makes a teacher a "caring teacher"?
6. How do you show care to your students?

"No person in the world ever lost anything by being nice to me."

LILLIE LANGTRY

Chapter 3

Because Teachers are Nice

Nice teachers were important to our survey respondents with an approval rating of 26.3%.

Maya Angelou once said, "I've learned that people will forget what you said, people will forget what you did, but people will never forget how you made them feel." I'd cite this. Bring to mind a kind person from your past. What was it about them that made your brain categorize them as "nice?" Chances are pretty good that they were positive and kind, and the simple thought of them makes you smile. Why is this? Why do these people stand out in our mind and why is "nice" important? Our grandmothers are nice (we hope). Your parents are "nice" (we hope). Your friends are "nice" (we hope). You get the picture. So, why does every two or three people out of ten remember "niceness" when you ask them about their teachers?

Consider this story to illustrate "niceness" as a key characteristic of memorable teachers:

> My third grade teacher was AMAZING! She truly let you know she cared about you and was always there to help. She took time to check-in on kids when they were absent from school

while they were sick. She made time to be outside on recess even when she was not on duty. She was also creative and really loved her job. As a result, her students LOVED her class!

Now think of someone that you do not know but you assume they are nice. But, how do you REALLY know? Why does your brain automatically assume they are a nice person? What is it about them that makes you feel like you will connect with them on some level?

Think of Dolly Parton. We have never met Dolly Parton; however, we LOVE Dolly Parton. The movies we have seen her in, the documentaries we have viewed, and the interviews that we have listened to make her seem like a very "nice" person. She reads children's stories every night online to anyone who welcomes her into their home. Why does she do this? Because she is *nice*. Plain and simple. She draws off her own life-long story and shares her love with the world. The thought of Dolly Parton makes us smile because we assume she is a very nice person. She is thoughtful, giving, and genuine. For these three reasons, "nice" can be defined, and it was defined that way by our survey respondents. So, how can Siegle (2020) shed some light on the relevance of "nice" taking shape in our memory system?

> Physiologically, kindness can positively change your brain. Being kind [nice] boosts serotonin and dopamine, which are neurotransmitters in the brain that give you feelings of satisfaction and well-being, and cause the pleasure/reward centers in your brain to light up. Endorphins, which are your body's natural pain killer, also can be released.

Your brain responds the same when you are nice to others or when others are nice to you. The saying, "You never have a second chance to make a good impression," or as we would change the saying in education, "You never have a second chance to make an impression on the first day of school," bodes true for characterizing what "nice" can be to students. This impression can be positive and the students look forward to returning on day two, or it can be negative and the students look and expect the same dread as the first day. The choice to create a positive or negative experience for the students is solely up to the teacher.

Most students have an innate expectation as to what school will be like each year. They may not be as familiar with the new teacher or new school, but they have an expectation of what school "is supposed to be" based on previous experience. But, those expectations hold true for both positive and negative experiences. If a student is typically "bored" in school, they expect it to be boring. If a student has nice teachers along the way and then meets a gargantuan, they hit panic mode and do not know how to typically respond.

Just like we have never met Dolly Parton, we assume she is exceptionally kind based on her genuineness and perceived kindness. Students entering a new school with an assumption that the experience will be as it was in the past can either help them or haunt them. Our brains make the connection that since Dolly Parton exhibits the same traits as nice people that we already know in our lives, we assume she is a nice person because our experiences predict future outcomes and perceptions about others. An abused child will look through the lens of abuse as how their "normal" is defined. Meeting nice people who want to help them is challenging for those who are abused because it resets their established normal.

Students do the same thing all the time; their brains make a connection with previous school or teacher experiences and so, in their minds, that is what school or how that teacher will be for that next year.

Dr. Eric Rossen, Director of Professional Development and Standards for the National Association of School Psychologists, presented in January, 2021, and mentioned how the brain is not necessarily stressed by nature. The prefrontal cortex is able to have plenty of blood flow and allows the brain to be more open, rational, and reasonable and is likely to retain information as information comes to the brain.

The brain is not naturally defensive. Sensory experiences cause such stressors to the brain. When the brain undergoes some sort of stress or trauma, the body's natural defense is to send the majority of one's blood to their large muscles, not the prefrontal cortex, and, therefore, limits the ability of someone to function or think rationally. In other words, "Under excess stress, we regress" (Rossen, 2021). In looking at a different model of how the brain functions, Dr. Stuart Shanker (n.d.), Research Professor Emeritus of Philosophy and Psychology at York University and the CEO of the MEHRIT Centre, Ltd. explains the "Triune Brain." This examines the brain and separates it into three sections:

> At the bottom is the Reptilian brain…: an ancient system that takes over when we are threatened. Above this sits a 'mammalian'…where strong emotions and urges are triggered, and all sorts of communicative and social mechanisms operate 'beneath the threshold of conscious awareness.' At the top resides the 'neocortex'…which makes it possible for us to think, plan, learn, speak, be aware of others and be self-aware. Movement can go both ways, depending on how much stress we're under. The calmer we are, the more the [neocortex] is in control. The greater the stress, the more the [mammalian brain] takes over. And in emergency situations (real or imagined) the [reptilian brain] is in total command.

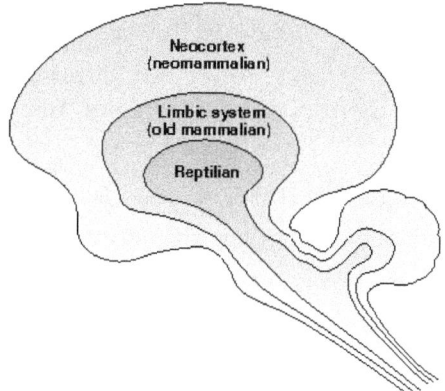

PAFCA, CC BY-SA 4.0 <https://creativecommons.org/licenses/by-sa/4.0>, via Wikimedia Commons

If a student is in a classroom where the teacher is not nice, students are likely to create a path in their brain which could be automatically triggering a pathway to fight or flight, rather than the path that allows the student to process, evaluate options, and plan appropriately to different situations. They may tend to be functioning in the red or brown areas of the brain--potentially not having control of their thinking, emotions, or outbursts that they may have in school.

Students who experienced the story below will positively remember their teacher because of the amount of adrenaline that pumped through their body at the mere mention of the teacher's name, let alone seeing them in person every day for an entire school year:

> I was chubby and many of the kids were mean to me. My teacher always encouraged me to believe in myself and my abilities. She did not let me obsess over my weight. She made me focus on my intelligence.

As former classroom teachers, we made it a point to get to know each and every one of our students. We needed to make sure that we knew multiple things about each student outside of school, so that we could connect with them.

"She seemed to care about all aspects of my day, not just school."

Notice how "caring" from the last chapter and "nice" go hand in hand here.

A principal of a high poverty elementary school had the entire staff come to a staff development hour with a notecard depicting the name of a student from their class on the card. The teachers put each of the cards on the tables in the library. The entire staff then walked around the room and wrote on the cards of the students if they knew something positive about that student outside of the school. Classroom teachers were not to respond to their own students. We see "nice" being defined as knowing something personally special about each child, and "niceness" flourished when "caring" attitudes are the center of a teacher's reason for being.

It was an eye-opening experience for the staff to see the significant number of students who did not have three facts written on many of the cards, unfortunately. They then split up the cards that had up to only two items written on them with each staff member taking a few cards each. It was their goal to connect with those students on a daily basis even if it was just to say, "Good morning, I'm so glad you are here today."

Each staff person had three to five students that they were to connect with outside of their regular classroom. This simple act increased attendance, decreased the amount of behavior issues, and led to more positive phone calls made home, and there were many more smiles around the school, from both the students and staff. Again, this is where "caring" and "nice" intersect.

But, then there is the role of negative name calling that is the converse of "niceness." One might say that the opposite of "nice" is "mean." Take a look at the simple sentence below:

He told me I was stupid and lazy. I have dyslexia and I struggled.

Think of *your* students now: How many of them have been identified with a learning or behavior disability? How many of them have gone undiagnosed? How many of these students have gone through school with mean teachers who did not realize that the students have special needs and truly want to do well, but yet have a mean teacher who makes them feel awful about their learning?

How many of these students have a nice teacher--one who reads the IEP and asks the appropriate questions on how to best teach these students because they truly care? How many of these students have a champion in their corner knowing that if they were tested, they may be able to better meet their individual needs?

How have the brains of those students above been impacted in either a negative or positive manner by the acts, or lack thereof, of kindness from their teachers?

I challenge you to think of a person who is **not** nice--someone who is actually just plain *mean*. Unfortunately, it is pretty easy to come up with a name and a face because those sensory experiences of loudness or cutting words enter into our compartmentalized brain, which stores them in memory centers for the rest of our lives. Look at the devastating recount below to see how this could scar that child's memory of teachers for life:

> *After two weeks of kindergarten, I was moved to a first grade class. It was a Friday and it was time for a spelling test. The teacher slapped a piece of paper down on the desk and said, 'If you're so smart, you can take the spelling test.' I remember crying (and failing the spelling test). I don't remember anything else about first grade.*

The effects of this incident on a child's brain is explained by Vandergriendt (2020): "Dopamine and serotonin are two neurotransmitters that play important roles in your brain and gut--they create an imbalance in your levels and either one can have effects on your mental health, digestion, and sleep cycle." Simply put: nice people mess with your brain in a good way and mean people mess with your brain in a terrible way.

In Rossen's (2021) presentation, "Preventing School from Becoming the 11th ACE," he mentions ten things (in no particular order) that teachers do which can cause trauma in students and could ultimately have a negative impact on the students' brains:

1. Low (or inconsistent) expectations
2. Negative relationships
3. Cultural insensitivity
4. Overly Punitive Discipline
5. Racism, Discrimination, and Inequity
6. Making Assumptions
7. No Access to Mental Health Supports
8. Trauma triggers (safety planning, environmental cues)
9. Insufficient family engagement and outreach
10. A stressed staff

Rossen points out that the teachers who exhibit any or all of the above-mentioned triggers might unknowingly cause students to experience trauma that lingers in the students' brains. In other words, when there is an absence of "niceness," other, more terrible things are happening inside of us that no one can see. Our brains are working overtime and meanness creates scarring.

I had a fifth grade teacher who slammed her hand on my desk and asked why I was so stupid.

In this case, the person who reported the above memory of their worst teacher forever stored the idea that this was not an effective form of teaching. What is truly unfortunate is that there are only two reasons for this teacher slamming her hand down on the student's desk asking them if "they are stupid": she either did not realize that this action was wrong or she purposely chose to be unkind to this student. Either way, that action made an imprint on this student's brain that identified the teacher as a their #1 *worst of all time* (WOAT) teacher.

A beautiful trait of most students is that they have the ability to sense if a person is genuinely nice and kind versus those who are faking. Being kind to students is vital--it makes a difference in their learning, in their lives, and in their future. It helps to define the person that they become--who they want to emulate. You are their role model.

As an educator, YOU can be kind to all: students, staff, and the community.

Why?

Because YOU are #1!

CHAPTER 3
BOOK STUDY
CHALLENGE

1. Go back to the person you brought to mind at the beginning of the chapter. Write down the attributes that make him/her "nice."
2. Take notice of your emotions while you write down these attributes. Then, place a star next to the attributes that you share in common with this person.
3. Put a checkmark by the attributes that you can improve upon in your school and/or class.
4. Have there been times when your kindness or niceness was fake? Explain.
5. What can you do to be more genuine with students?
6. How do you define "nice" thoughts, beliefs, and actions in your classroom or school?
7. Do you have open discussions about what it means to be "nice" with fellow staff members? Why or why not?

"If you think that you are too small to make a difference, try sleeping with a mosquito!"

DALAI LAMA

Chapter 4

Because Teachers Are Funny

F unny teachers were important to our survey respondents with an approval rating of 34.8%.

"Comedy is very controlling – you are making people laugh."

— Gilda Radner

Think of a joke, any joke --maybe one that you tell often. (No dirty jokes, please).

Three cats named Un, Deux, and Trois, Quatre (One, Two, Three, Four) walk across a bridge. As they get to the top, the bridge breaks and the cats fall into the water. What happened next? Un, Deux, Trois, Quatre, Cinq. (Meaning One, Two, Three, Four cats, "sank.")

This terribly cheesy joke was taught for many acadian generations and then repeated by a French teacher for centuries. Why is this remembered? Why did the mind retain this exceptionally cheesy joke but yet, when one retells it now, creates a smile whether it is silly, cheesy, or just plain dumb. Yet, close to 35% of our survey respondents believe that humorous teachers are even more important than nice teachers! Why?

According to Scott Edwards from Harvard Mahoney Neuroscience Institute (2010):

> The path of neuronal activity is a complex one that enlists various brain regions: the frontal lobe, to process the information; the supplementary motor area, to tap learned experience to direct motor activities such as the movements associated with laughter; and the nucleus accumbens, to assess the pleasure of the story and the reward that the 'aha!' brings. When the punchline hits home, your heart rate rises, you jiggle with mirth, and your brain releases 'feel good' neurotransmitters: dopamine, serotonin and an array of endorphins.

Humor has incredible brain power!

Mrs. Sheehy came to school every day prepared and ready. She had a sense of humor and was a consummate professional. She loved the high school students and she could make you feel like the most important person in the room. I did not feel like I found success in school until I took classes with her because she made me laugh . . . she made my day!

Being in Mrs. Sheehy's room, regardless of what she taught, made her students happy. Her sense of humor and the fact that the students knew she loved being there, released the "feel good" neurotransmitters to which the Harvard Mahoney Neuroscience Institute (2010) was referring to and it doesn't end there. These neurotransmitters are released in the brains of the students and the teacher! Let's look deeper at the implications of humor on the brain:

> Studies have shown that the prefrontal cortex plays a vital role in the flexible thinking required to 'get' a joke. This region of the frontal

lobe, located forward of the brain's motor regions, processes sensory information gathered by our eyes, ears, and other senses, then combines this information in a manner that helps us form useful, behavior-guiding judgments. The region also oversees the processing needed for planning complex cognitive behaviors, showing personality characteristics, and moderating social behavior. And it is the prefrontal cortex that helps us make sense of a joke's punch line by sending signals along connections to both the supplementary motor area and the nucleus accumbens, producing a strong sense of surprise and eliciting laughter. In short, our prefrontal cortex is on the case as soon (as soon as we start hearing the joke) (Harvard Mahoney Neuroscience Institute, 2010).

Hence why we start smiling as soon as the joke begins!

In essence, if you want to wake up the brains of those you are teaching, tell a joke and make them laugh! Not only will this wake up their brains so they are ready to create the synapses that are required to learn and retain knowledge, it will also help with classroom management and lessen behavior problems. Who can be naughty when they are enjoying learning?

We are not contending that the best teachers are just the funniest teachers. What we are saying, however, is that humor not only has incredible brain triggers, but it came out as an incredibly high elemental characteristic in our research. And, no, we are not saying that teachers have to dance around the classroom like circus clowns or find a joke of the day that everyone sees as dry or unentertaining.

But, if a teacher were to have **no** sense of humor, they would not intrigue the brain to want to learn. Where there is entertainment, there is often humor. Consider this story below:

> *I had a college sociology professor who did nothing but stood in front of the class and read to us from the sociology book. No lecture, no conversa-*

tion, no dialog, just read to us from the book. I don't remember anything from the class except that he stood in the front with the book on the podium and in a monotone voice read from the psychology book. All I could think of was the Economics teacher. I am pretty sure if he smiled once, he would have cracked his face. It was our internal jokes about 'Stale Dale' that made the class memorable.

If you had the option of sitting in to observe Mrs. Sheehy's class or "Stale Dale's" class, which would you prefer? It's obvious, of course, yet, we do not explicitly make humor an obvious element in our teaching each day. You might be thinking, "Well, I'm just not that funny. I'm a good teacher, but I'm just not funny." But, what if we told you that YOU will more likely be engaged, smile, laugh and enjoy learning, yourself, when you try to find the humor in life? We are not asking you to become a circus clown, but there are ways to instill humor in your teaching methods and style even if you simply invite humor to drop in on you each day. Your students could take charge in humorous things or put together ways to make learning more humorous.

Humor has a few characteristics that stuck out to us in our research while listening to others stories:

1. Humor is not meant to be manufactured. Humor occurs naturally.
2. Humor does not mean "sarcasm." We all know that sarcasm is often a tactic of bullying.
3. Humor is supposed to suit one's personality; it is not meant to change our personalities.

A learner will not benefit from our instruction unless they actively attend to us and humor captures such active attention and novelty:

Attention is enhanced when neuromodulators like acetylcholine and norepinephrine are stimulated through educational interaction that is engaging with some novelty. We might call this the *wow* factor. Teachers can enhance attention by simply maintaining eye contact, moving around the classroom, interacting with students and assuring that before any instruction, the students are engaged, (Burns, 2019).

They can also use humor to get the same effect from students!
Think of your classroom and the students who fill the seats. We all know the toll that anxiety, depression, and other mood disorders take on many of our students. The devastation that is caused in the brain of those who have experienced trauma is exceptional. This is not only the case for the students, but for the adults, as well. But, what if there was a way for you to help alleviate some of the effects of the trauma they have experienced? What if there was a way to benefit all who are in the classroom: teacher and students? There is a way: laugh!

You know the saying, "Laughter is the best medicine." There is scientific evidence to prove this. A Harvard study conducted in 2004 demonstrated the effect that laughter had on patients who were being treated for depression, anxiety and other mood disorders. Take a look at this:

> To determine whether laughter had an effect on the patients, Marci measured the skin conductance, basically a measure of sweat, of both patients and psychiatrists. Skin conductance increases with the nervous system activity that controls blood pressure and heart rate, which together signal an aroused state. When clinicians did not laugh with patients, conductance measures still indicated both parties were aroused. But when patients and psychiatrists laughed together, the arousal measures for each group doubled...the contagion of laughter, suggests that patients felt that the emotions they expressed were being validated. (Edwards, 2010)

Humor, therefore, is remembered, forever, and in the case of **YOU ARE #1**, you, too can see the power of how humor can transform your classroom into an active classroom:

> *In addition to being kind, funny, and excited about both his subject AND his students, he NEVER failed to treat us like human beings...he was a man of empathy, compassion, and understanding. This man was my Spanish teacher, my favorite teacher. I was so incredibly fortunate to have him. To this day, thirty days into my career as a teacher, his example informs everything I do in the classroom. I stole his approach, his jokes and even his mannerisms.*

This Spanish teacher made learning fun and memorable. The way he taught will always play a role in this new teacher's life. His legacy is being passed to this new teacher's students. He likely is the reason why this teacher went into the profession. This new teacher made the decision to be just like his favorite teacher, and modeling his sense of humor, this new teacher is likely going to be the #1 favorite teacher of many other students' top three teachers of all time.

Unfortunately, the brain also fires up when an inappropriate or bad joke is made. How? Well, the brain waits for a "punchline" which, therefore, opens the pathways to the other parts of the brain--only to register it as a bad experience. This causes an increased cortisol level, causing a memory to be made, however, and not a pleasant one:

> *I had a teacher who appeared to seek approval from the jocks and cheerleaders in school. He told jokes that were not funny or were borderline inappropriate. He wasted class time, almost like he expected us to teach ourselves Geometry so he could talk about what was going on in sports or the personal lives of SOME students. Even the jocks and cheerleaders who appeared to be his favorites did not respect him.*

In an attempt to be "cool," this teacher caused the majority of his students to remember him as the #1 worst teacher on many levels: he demonstrated favoritism, failed to try and relate to more than just the student athletes, and tried to use bad humor as an attempt to make others laugh. How unfortunate to not receive respect from anyone, even the students he tried to appease.

So what happens to the teacher's brain when they try to be funny? USC doctoral student Ori Amir and Irving Biederman (2016), a professor of psychology and computer science, led a group of students from the University of Southern California to research just that. Their objective was to see how the brain's physiology changes when a person tries to be funny by studying comedians.

> The path of neuronal activity is a complex one that enlists various brain regions: the frontal lobe, to process the information; the supplementary motor area, to tap learned experience to direct motor activities such as the movements associated with laughter; and the nucleus accumbens, to assess the pleasure of the story and the reward that the 'aha!' brings. When the punchline hits home, your heart rate rises, you jiggle with mirth, and your brain releases 'feel good' neurotransmitters: dopamine, serotonin and an array of endorphins (Boston, 2017).

Essentially, being funny includes almost every aspect of the brain and triggers hormones that make the body feel "good."

The study also showed that the temporal lobe regions that are activated from humor and laughter are also activated by the "aesthetic experience of appreciating a magnificent vista," meaning the areas aroused by visual recognition. The brain is activated to learn new material at this time. According to the study, "humans are hardwired to crave new information and experiences." Humor and laughter help the brain to open up to these new experiences.

> One can actually see what humor does in the brain. In the past, scientists have studied the neural correlates of creativity with tasks such as

writing a poem, improvising jazz or drawing a picture, but humor offered a unique pathway to study how the brain processes creation. Humor is an outstanding testbed for studying creativity; it has a clear beginning, middle and end with a duration brief enough for neuroimaging. Also, the end product is easy to evaluate: Does it make you laugh?

Here's something that we hope gives you an end-of-chapter chuckle:

> Student: "Would you punish me for something that I didn't do?"
> Teacher: "Of course not!"
> Student: "Good, because I didn't do my homework!"

Why did this joke make you chuckle even if it is a cheesy joke? Maybe, it was an attempt to brighten someone's day. Maybe it was a way to connect with someone through a lens of mocking oneself. Maybe it is . . .

Because YOU are #1!

CHAPTER 4
BOOK STUDY CHALLENGE

1. What makes you laugh?
2. What kind of sense of humor do you have?
3. Do you think that your sense of humor comes across to your students? Why/Why not?
4. Tell one joke in your school every day for a month and notice the difference in the atmosphere of the classroom. Find a good one right now to use tomorrow. In fact, look up 10 jokes right now and write them down so you have two weeks worth to get you going.
5. Create the joke in a manner that ties into what is being taught or discussed and see what the retention of the material is among your students or staff.

"Happiness is excitement that has found a settling down place, but there is always a little corner that keeps flapping around."

E. L. KONIGSBURG

Chapter 5

Because Teachers are Exciting

Exciting teachers were important to our survey respondents with an approval rating of 35.4%.

In the movie, *Ferris Bueller's Day Off*, Ben Stein played an economics teacher at Ferris' high school. In one epic scene, the monotone Stein rambled on and on answering his own questions after asking, "Anyone . . . anyone . . .?" while kids drooled on their desks as they slept or chewed bubble gum to see just how big their bubbles could really get. Disinterested, boring, and borderline flatlined, Stein depicts the type of teacher we've all had: Unexciting!

The thing about having exciting teachers is that some (maybe of the more boring pool of) teachers feel that school is not a place where we should dance around like actors on the stage of an unrealistic life. Some say, "But, the students will not always have fun things to do in class and we have to prepare them for the real world."

The real world of what? Boredom?

Imagine a school where all of your former teachers were excited about teaching and were exciting to be around. Imagine a place where you were actually interested in attending because you were going to be entertained into learning something for the rest of your lives. If memorable teachers can make learning memorable, then the same goes true for the converse: Boring teachers will have the power to bore you to the point where you don't remember anything about science or social studies.

Right?

Possibly.

Our survey respondents, while answering the question, "What makes a teacher a good teacher or a memorable teacher," felt that excitement was important, but only under certain circumstances. They wouldn't have felt that it could make the top tier of characteristics in teachers that also work heavily on the sensory components of our memory--which we have discussed at the start of this book. If teachers do something exciting in their science lab or act out a scene in *Romeo and Juliette* that we will remember forever, there is a good chance that we will remember that teacher forever, too, and maybe even strive to be just like them someday.

But, be careful, here. If you have an exciting teacher who also makes fun of a student, that will have a lasting memory in the negative zone of memory recall. We've seen this happen; you might have seen this, as well.

Let us illustrate this major point.

Mr. Ewing, a superb teacher, was equally excited about throwing a student out of class while he was teaching *A Clockwork Orange* in his senior English 12 seminar. When he pushed this student into the hallway and threw a desk out into the hallway afterwards, yes (probably meaning to hit him), that was memorable, indeed. But no, I will not think of Mr. Ewing as an impressionable teacher in the positive unless I like violence and thought that this was a cool thing to do. For many, Mr. Ewing will be remembered, but he will be remembered for throwing a desk at a student and Mr. Ewing will not be an instant positive memory. He will be the antithesis of how we want people to remember their teachers for and for what characteristics teachers can really be positively remembered. Mr. Ewing taught in a world of teaching which was different from what we know now. He taught when corporal punishment was not eradicated in school systems, and where punishment of this nature was allowed.

Yes, those negative memories will last a lifetime, but the positive ones carry more punch. So, I ask you: If YOU had an education filled with exciting teachers and they were EVERYWHERE in your school, would you have turned out differently than you did today? Maybe? If not, you still may have gone to school more, done better on tests, not wanted to play sick in order to stay home, or lived to tell the stories of these amazing people who love to turn up the throttle of excited learning unlike Ben Stein.

So, what is the magic behind excitement? Is it all fluff and no substance? Is it getting off topic and telling powerful stories? Is it jumping around and acting like a fool to prove a point in class? Well, maybe some of this creates memorable teachers, but for the most part, there are four major ways, according to our research, that create exciting, memorable teachers (in the positive).

Teachers Who Make Students Come Alive

We've seen it millions of times: A student is disengaged from school. Their head is down on their desk. They don't look the teacher in the eye. You may see this same student in another teacher's classroom fully engaged, excited, and the reason why they want to come to school in the first place.

Some of these disengaged students are borderline flatline and perhaps filled with shyness. School is a place where anxiety fills every part of their body. Until . . . that teacher makes them come alive. See, it is the part of the teacher recognizing that they are going to try to make that student come alive, which is the interesting part of *YOU ARE #1*.

Teachers are plagued with paperwork upon paperwork each day. Course loads that make a day absolutely exhausting result in coming home and flopping down on the couch. It is the teachers who recognize the withdrawn who are true champions, and according to those who responded to our survey, teachers who made them come alive while they were at school topped the list of those who were memorable to them.

Good teachers, great ones for that matter, fight the good fight of trying to brainwash students with messages that transport a positive notion of themselves--a sort of self-esteem building crash course filled with care. What if a teacher told you each day that you were a winner, not a loser, and to not let anyone tell you any differently. See, the brain registers this kind of brainwashing time and time again into belief systems that are created rather than disbelief systems that fail our students. Brainwashing and sending positive messages of propaganda can change a child's life in the present and stay with them in the future.

When teachers get excited about turning around the life of a youth, this not only changes the world of schooling for that child, it also changes their life, forever.

Teachers Who Make Content Come Alive

Take a typical boring math class. We are picking on math because it can be incredibly boring for many students. To be an exhilarating math teacher is one of the toughest jobs on the planet. Yet, there are master teachers out there who make math easily understandable and exciting!

You might be reading this and thinking that we are being hard on math teachers. Actually, it is just the opposite. What if you asked students two questions about math and their math teacher:

1. Do you like math?
2. Do you like your math teacher?

These basic level questions can mean a world of difference to students and teachers all over the planet. Obviously, the idea here (and with all subjects in school) is to get a firm "yes" to both of those questions, right? Maybe. But, maybe not, either. If a student loves their teacher, they will do just about anything for them. Conversely, if a student loves math, but hates their teacher, they feel awful about having to see that teacher, but will still do the math to pass, most likely.

Consider the story of Mrs. Barker . . .

On a typical day in a typical school, the quadratic equation needed to be taught to Mrs. Barker's 9th graders. She knew that it was a boring lesson, but didn't want to settle for boredom. In fact, Mrs. Barker loved the quadratic equation much like an accountant loves spreadsheets and filling in budget numbers. They are a different breed, but they love their craft, indeed!

So the quadratic formula was what needed to be accomplished and Mrs. Barker anticipated that her students would be bored, for sure. While listening to her playlist, Mrs. Barker noticed herself tapping her foot to Drake's "God's Plan." She knew that her students loved the song too.

"That's it!" She thought.

Mrs. Barker changed the lyrics to "God's Plan" and called it "God's Math." That would be her anticipatory set to get the kids ready for an increased message of "math is heavenly." Check out her revisions below and imagine her singing the tune while her students walked into the classroom and she passed the lyrics out to get them fired up about math.

God's Math
(adapted from Drake's God's Plan)
Yeah division, addition, division, addition
Division on me, yuh
I been movin' digits, start no trouble with me
Tryna solve it right is a struggle for me

Don't pull up at 6 AM with math homework for me
You know how I like math when you testing me
I don't wanna sub all the numbers you see
Yes I see the formula they pushin on me
Hope I got some answers that come easy for me
They gon' tell the story, math was different with me
God's math, God's math
I hold back, sometimes I won't, yuh
I feel good, sometimes I don't, ayy,
I solved numbers, anyway, yo
Might go down as M-A-T-H
I go hard on showin' work, yuh, Way
I make sure that math work come my way, eh
And still
Math things
It's a lot of Math things
Yeah division, addition, division, addition
Division on me
Yuh, ayy, ayy (ayy)
She says, "Do you love me?" I tell her, "Only partly"
I only love my math and my momma, I'm sorry . . .

And . . . it worked!

Mrs. Barker's students were laughing and singing along while plugging in values to the quadratic formula. This is where humor, discussed in the last chapter, intersects with excitement. Mrs. Barker *was* Drake not only in that moment, but, forever, in her students' memories. She made the content come alive to something that was drop-dead boring for many. And that makes a good teacher an exciting teacher!

Teachers Who are EXCITED about what They Teach

Mrs. Barker loved math, yes, but how many times have you come across a teacher who doesn't feel much of anything when teaching their subject content?

In the movie, *Back to School,* starring Rodney Dangerfield, Professor Turgeson, played by Sam Kinison, was not only passionate about teaching the Vietnam War and the Korean Conflict, but borderline insane while having flashbacks of his army service while teaching (Metter, 1986, 1:36:00). Of course, we are not recommending that you call your students names or break a desk while you teach, but there is something to be said about the passion that Professor Turgeson had for his content, his craft.

So, what if our students loved our subjects taught just as much as we love them? Can we make teaching and learning with passion and excitement an epidemic among our students? Well, the research that we collected said that teachers who loved what they taught were remembered positively for the rest of their lives.

Consider the story of Mr. Kowalski:

Mr. Kowalski loved teaching home and careers. He loved cooking and he loved eating too! To accomplish having students bake a breakfast quiche, Mr. Kowalski dressed up like Gordon Ramsey, showed a *Hell's Kitchen* clip, and then taught his students how a failed dish might look versus a successful dish. With egg shells peppered into his egg mix, he threw the bowl out the window like Ramsey may have done and started all over. His students were perplexed! They had a blast learning not only how to bake a perfect quiche, but how to mess it up, as well. Teaching missteps was a way for Mr. Kowalski to get through to his students and the love that Mr. Kowalski had for cooking came through each and every day that he went to work. Mr.Kowalski was memorable, to say the least.

Teachers Who are EXCITED About What They Do

Some of the best teachers whom we have met are all-consuming teachers. In other words, teaching is not just a job or a profession. It is a *way of life* for a teacher who is remembered, forever. They LOVE sharing what they learn. They love telling students where they found a resource or how a concept that they are teaching relates to something in their lives. They live for teaching and teach in order to live life to its fullest. They adore the profession and wake up each morning thinking about their students and ways to get through to them.

Whether telling students about a book that you read (maybe even sharing **YOU ARE #1** with them) or a course that you took or a conference that you attended or a podcast that you listened to, getting your students in the loop about your own growth-excitement is something that lasts with students, forever.

Moving from your own growth-excitement, turning that into a passion for life-long learning, and then modeling what a life-long learner looks like is crucial for students of today. It is important for students to learn how to always be students of tomorrow--no matter if they are auto mechanics, electricians, physicians, or waiters. Learning new skills for any and all professions or jobs is something that never ends.

Why?

Because YOU are #1!

CHAPTER 5
BOOK STUDY CHALLENGE

1. In what ways do you make students come alive in school each day? What do you actually do? Be specific.
2. How do you make your content come alive and be exciting for students?
3. How do your students know that you love teaching?
4. How can you show students that you love teaching what you teach?
5. How can you share your love of the profession of teaching with your students?
6. What are some physical ways and subliminal ways that you can demonstrate teacher excitement?

"Without involvement, there is no commitment. Mark it down, asterisk it, circle it, underline it. No involvement, no commitment."

STEPHEN COVEY

Chapter 6

Because Teachers are Involved

Teachers who are involved were important to our survey respondents with an approval rating of 62.1%.

But, what does "involved" actually mean?

Humans have a need for involvement at any age and in any way. How this looks for some is different than others, but they still have a desire to be involved. This can be demonstrated in a plethora of ways: a grandparent who wants to hear from their very busy grandchildren or who takes the time out of their lives to go to their grandchild's softball game, the high school student who has to get good grades so they can stay involved in football, the overbearing helicopter parent who has to be in the classroom every day so they know what is going on, or the elementary school student who cannot wait to get the birthday invitation from someone. They all want to be involved and to have others want to be involved with them. Why? Because we care and we want others to care about us. But, involvement, such as the helicopter parent or even a teacher who is getting TOO involved in their students' lives by way of becoming involved in school-wide rumors or who a student is dating--these are *destructive* ways of being involved.

We remember our #1 teachers because they took the time to be involved with us in a positive way, not a creepy way or over-involved way. Breaking down the research that was presented to us, we found positive involvement to mean three different things to our research respondents:

1. Involvement in the lives of students was important to them.
2. Involvement in the achievement of students was important to them.
3. Involvement included the ideals of advocacy for education at local, state, and federal levels.

Take a look at the sentence below:

Mrs. Olsen treated us as if we were a part of her family.

"Family" means a sense-of-belonging, not a strange relationship that a teacher has with their students. A three-year study conducted by students at the University of Girona demonstrated a clearer picture of involvement:

> *Involvement* concerns the desire to form and maintain strong and stable interpersonal relationships. Teachers can be involved by showing affection and interest, by being empathetic, by promoting pro-social behavior in class, by being available to all students, and by showing commitment to students' learning. Four components of teacher involvement are distinguished: First, teachers can express their involvement by showing affection; Second, teachers can express their attunement to the student by showing that they understand him/her; Third, teachers can provide resources (e.g., time) to the student; and Fourth, teachers can make sure that they are dependable and available to offer support. (Ayllon, Alsina, & Colomer, 2019)

We are going to look at these four identified areas to further delve into how teachers' involvement impacts the learning and motivation of their students while acknowledging the two components that our own research pointed to and is in direct alignment with Ayllon et al.'s (2019) work.

Showing Affection

As former classroom teachers, we have fond memories of looking at the faces behind the desks and could not stop ourselves from loving each and every one of those faces. Then, as we knew more and more about our students, we quickly found out who had at least one family member who was involved in their school and their lives and those who did not have anyone. Although we cared deeply for each of our students, we found that those who did not get to go home to a hug or a parent or guardian who would ask "How was your day?" became those students who were given attention and greetings, such as "I'm so glad you're here today."

Some students needed extra caring and extra love and this is further supported by Wentzel and Ramani (2016):

> Emotional supportive teacher-student relationships that lack continued levels of high conflict are conducive to student learning and are of particular importance for at-risk students…it is clear that teachers should focus on creating warm and not conflictual relationships and be sensitive to their students' needs. High levels of teacher communion and agency, offering relatedness and strengthening students' belief in their competence are characteristics of such relationships (138).

Involvement means that a genuine capacity of wanting to help in any way without mixed messages or forced relationships outside of school is crucial to a student's memory creation, forever. Some students ask teachers to be their mentors. Others look at their teachers as parent figures that they never had. Most teachers remembered for involvement are the ones who advocate for their students in some major way. The story below illustrates the role that advocacy plays:

> *When I was in 1st grade, administration wanted to send me to another school and my teacher stood up for me telling them it wasn't best for me. During summer vacation, she called my parents directly to talk with them. I was no longer her student, I would always be one of her "kids."*

Unlike this teacher, the #1 worst teachers are the ones who are not involved and create a learning environment that is hostile, cold, uncaring, and uncomfortable. They do not advocate for their students and show no care in their success, either in school or outside of school. These teachers are the ones who make students feel unwelcome. Consider the story below:

> *I had a classmate with very limited resources and a very difficult home situation. Our teacher was unkind to him. She pointed out his tattered clothes (limited, ill fitting, overworn), shoes that did not fit, how he was often tardy (his family had no working vehicle) and he often did not complete any homework. The child was lost in so many ways and his teacher was not only terrible to him each day, but he was uninvolved and absent as a caring human being who should stick up for those who cannot help themselves.*

Imagine what it was like for this child who couldn't count on his teacher for anything--even if it was just some mercy on outstanding homework assignments.

Empathy as a Component of Emotional Involvement

In the movie *Freedom Writers (LaGravenese, 2007, 2:02:00)*, Hillary Swank portrays a teacher named, Erin Gruwell, who teaches English for at-risk students at Woodrow Wilson High School--a once highly acclaimed school that declined since voluntary integration had become voluntary. Racial tension increased since the Los Angeles riots happened two years prior to the contextualized release of the film. Erin struggled to form a connection with her students and observed numerous fights among them, some who were in rival gangs.

Desperate to find a connection with her students, Erin used activities such as games and field trips, in order to better understand her students. Erin had them write about their lives in journals. These entries helped her to better understand her students, connect with her students, become involved in their lives and educational success, and better equipped her to support them in ways that they could not have imagined.

If you've ever had the distinct pleasure of meeting Manny Scott, an exceptional author, a riveting motivational speaker, and one of the original Freedom Writers, you know what it is like to listen to him speak. He talks about the "Power of One." How one teacher made the difference in his life, how one teacher helped turn his life around, how one teacher put him on the path to success--all because time was taken by his teacher to understand him and his classmates. All it takes is one teacher to make a difference in a student's life, forever.

Furthermore, involvement also relies on perspective seeking by a teacher. Take a look at what Sparks (2019) explains about the role of perspective seeking as a foundational building block for empathy which can lead to high involvement:

> Across several recent studies, researchers have found that teachers who cultivate empathy for and with their students are able to manage students' behavior and academic engagement better. Trying to suppress

biases or stereotypes about students can sometimes make them worse, but practicing perspective-taking--the role of actively imagining how a student might perceive or be affected by a situation--can reduce bias and deepen teacher-student relationships.

This type of involvement which is based on empathy and perspective seeking is one of the reasons why people who've had incredible teacher then go on to *become* a teacher, themselves:

I had the privilege of working with my brother's special education teacher at church. We talked a lot about helping students be ready to learn, and she always saw ways to help students who often failed to find their ways to succeed and even excel. Because of her, I became a special education teacher.

It is incredible to us that a #1 teacher who wasn't even this person's teacher had the power to make such a direct impact to the point where this teacher will always be a role model for this person. Seeing the power of empathy and the impact that it has on others created a new level of empathy that will be carried on. Who knows? Maybe one of their students will see this and carry it on even further.

Education does not only include reading, writing and math. **Education and teaching also include teaching students how to make good choices, turn bad choices around, and be good human beings.** Teachers have a responsibility to own their actions and share personal stories of their choices: good and bad, and how they overcame obstacles. Having these conversations helps the students understand the teacher, and therefore this connection will help the students realize they are also being understood.

Later, we will talk more about the role of identifying with or understanding our students, but here, understanding is a cornerstone of empathy which can lead to high involvement by teachers everywhere:

This teacher told us personal and inspiring stories to teach us life lessons. She continually engaged us in conversation and dialogue that had meaning. She had high expectations of us to be good human beings and cared about us beyond only academic excellence.

Being Available to Students

"The greatest gift you can give someone is your TIME. Because when you give your time, you are giving a portion of your life that you will never get back."

— Anonymous

Connecting to students outside of the classroom is imperative to their learning. Many good teachers strive to attend at least one activity that each of their students participate in: sports games and meets, drama performances, band and chorus recitals, etc. If students are involved in something, anything, it is highly memorable if their teacher has attended.

The University of Girona conducted a study on what mattered most when it came to the success of higher education students (Ayllon et al., 2019). The study found that involvement was crucial to success and achievement because it builds a relationship beyond the classroom:

> What matters for college students' achievement is not so much *structure* or *autonomy support*, but rather the teacher's *involvement* in the student learning process and students' feelings of competence (*self-efficacy*), as measured by the impression students have that they are helped when questions arise, are learning, and are able to prove that they are learning. Our findings are relevant and novel in the context of higher education, as they provide new knowledge that contributes to a more nuanced understanding of the psychological needs of university

students to improve their motivation and performance, and of the degree to which self-efficacy triggers the learning process (Ayllon).

Here, involvement is an investment of time, and time is a conscious choice of good teachers who wish to influence their students in a positive manner. Consider this brief story plotline:

I came from a very dysfunctional family and the teacher brought me lunch daily. She also went the extra mile to let me stay at her house on Friday or Saturday so that I could participate in the school drama production.

Nowadays, this would be frowned upon, but we are in a different age than when this took place and a time when this may not have been looked upon as legally murky. While nothing ever was inappropriate in this example, it illustrates doing something to combat poverty and broken homes.

Today, teachers may show up early to meet the student and make the school showers available to these students and provide them with clean clothes from the "Care Closet" in the school. Providing time is a selfless giving of one's self, the only resource that you cannot ever get back. The gift of time can make a significant difference in the lives of your students, and it was highly revered in our research for **YOU ARE #1**.

Unfortunately, there are some teachers who are not willing to give extra of themselves. These teachers are regularly identified as uninvolved and rated for their quality strictly because they were uninvolved. It is interesting that something so simple can have incredible positive (or negative) impacts on the memories that we hold about our teachers.

A teacher's "contract mindset" can have lasting negative impacts on their students, forever:

I had a third grade teacher who refused to open her door to the students that arrived at school before the bell rang. She told us that her contract stated that she did not have to. So while all of the other teachers were working with their students who were dropped off by the bus before the bell, our class had to wait in line outside her closed door. Thankfully the other teachers would often take us in their class.

Showing Commitment to Student Achievement

Individualized instruction is more than a common catch-phrase. It has to be the norm in any classroom. Each student is unique and comes to us from a unique place. While we may all have the same academic standards that students all have to meet, how they learn those standards and then demonstrate that they understand the material, that is the art of education. How does this occur? Having a classroom teacher who is fully committed to the students' learning and is willing to do whatever they can to meet the needs of the students they teach. Take a look at how Lynch (2015) illustrates the role that commitment to teaching and achievement is a powerful attribute to involved teachers:

> While a classroom is one large group by design, it is made of many unique individuals with unique needs. You can meet learners' needs by providing a variety of teaching methods, including direct instruction, grouping students, and rearranging the groups as needed. To reach the individual student, you must strive to motivate each individual, involve him or her in learning, and understand how to teach everyone, not simply aim to teach the average student. You must also be an advocate for your students as individuals, ensuring that they have all the resources they need to succeed.

Are there times when a teacher has a meeting, an appointment, or a reason that they cannot always be available? Of course! This is life. However, it is the impression that the teacher is always available that makes the difference in the minds and memories of the teachers. The students will always remember how the teachers make them feel as depicted in this story below:

> *My senior English and homeroom teacher helped me become more involved in school. High school English was really tough for me and was just killing me. But, my teacher never let us quit. He taught and encouraged us until we got it. He always offered extra assistance and I will always remember that.*

The teachers who give of themselves and do what they can to meet the students' academic needs makes a difference. It makes them a #1 teacher, just like this:

> *She was always uplifting and positive. She knew I struggled academically but continued to gently push me. Toward the end of the year, she chose to submit one of **my** writing pieces to our county's writing contest. I did not win the award, but I did consider myself a winner because she saw my true potential.*

The teachers who are involved with their students by showing affection, being empathetic, being available, and making a commitment to their students all create a place in their students' brains that will be remembered, forever.
Why?

Because YOU are #1!

CHAPTER 6
BOOK STUDY
CHALLENGE

1. Did you have any teachers who were involved in your life inside or outside of school?

2. How involved are you with all of your students?

3. How interested are you in your students' lives outside of education?

4. How much time do you invest on your students outside of your contracted hours?

5. How involved do you want to be or are allowed to be without putting yourself at risk within your career?

Choose one of the following strategies to try for one month:

1. Find out the outside interests of your students (e.g. what sport teams they are on, what concerts or performances they will be in) and attend as many events as possible. Monitor your relationships with the students that you become involved with by taking an interest in their lives.
2. Talk to each of your students and celebrate the "something" unique to them--perhaps, one student per day.
3. Create a "Who We Are" wall where each student writes about themselves, what they like, what interests they have, whatever they want others to know about them.

"Most of your suffering comes from the lack of understanding of yourself and others."

THICH NHAT HANH

Chapter 7

Because Teachers Understand

Having understanding teachers was important to our survey respondents with an approval rating of 19.2%.

This chapter may seem similar to Chapter 2 (which is about caring) and Chapter 3 (which is about being nice), but it is actually *completely* different. Understanding doesn't have to mean a teacher can relate to what a student went through or is going through, but of course, it most certainly can. Some of the best teachers we've seen cannot possibly understand where their students come from, how they experience the world from their own plight or perspective, or even how poverty or wealth can impact a student's life viewpoint. We don't have to come from the same neighborhood to be understanding, nor do we have to have the same skin color or heritage.

> *Mr. Lewis was a memorable teacher because he was understanding. He would listen patiently, let students cry as hard as they needed to when they were hurting, and offered advice only when he was asked. He was a comfort to his students because he was a powerful listener and then responded to the situation or problem at hand with directness and motivation.*

By showing that we honestly care, we are modeling for our students how to do the same for others.

One day, Mr. Lewis was approached by Jesse, one of his seniors, after class. Jesse told him that she wasn't going to graduate--that she had to go to work to support her family and her sick brother. She cried and cried and was hopelessly helpless all at the same time. Mr. Lewis knew what he had to do.

He told Jesse that he dropped out of high school because he hated school. He didn't know what it was like to want to graduate and not be able to; instead, he only could speak from his own experience which was just the opposite. He couldn't wait to turn sixteen so he could drop out.

Yet, both Jesse and Mr. Lewis' stories are similar in a way. Both felt or will feel a loss and a new barrier that will have to be overcome. Getting a Graduation Equivalency Diploma (GED) will be Jesse's next hurdle or will it?

Mr. Lewis had an idea: What if he loaned Jesse a school laptop and she could do her work from home after work? In the age of virtual and hybrid learning, this is now a no-brainer for educators across the globe. Jesse couldn't believe her ears. Yes! It could work!

The identification that Mr. Lewis had with Jesse was not exactly the same, and we contend that it doesn't have to be in *You Are #1*. But, Mr. Lewis related to Jesse by listening, identifying with (whether it was directly or indirectly), and being flexible in the situation that strictly advocated for a student. And, THAT makes Mr. Lewis #1 and, forever, memorable by Jesse!

Teachers Who Understand (by Listening)

Margot went to Mrs. Williams to tell her that she was coming to believe that she is transgender. She'd spent years feeling isolated in school and society. She also claimed to Mrs. Williams that she was getting far away from God ever since she was thirteen. Now that she is a junior in high school, Margot wants to become who she really is.

Mrs. Williams was very surprised. She had never seen signs of Margot's struggle with her gender and identity. Margot seemed like a "typical girl." She was a good student and her grades remained high. Mrs. Williams remembered Margot taking pride in her Latino heritage and standing up for others who were bullied in school. She saw nothing on the outside that would hint at the huge struggle Margot had been having on the inside.

All Mrs. Williams could do, at first, was listen. She archived their conversation in her mind and remembered all of the details to this day. A Christian, herself, she could identify with the Lord and what being a Christian means to her. But she had absolutely no experience with the gender identity struggle Margot was going through. So, she decided to listen in order to come up with a series of questions, not necessarily solutions.

What Margot needed at that moment in time was a non-judgmental listener and Margot found that in Mrs. Williams. Another sentence that seems important enough to call out in some way. She was able to dump everything on her mind and get everything off of her chest. She didn't ask Mrs. Williams many questions; she just talked and talked about how she felt and exclaimed that she didn't know what to do.

Sometimes, *all we can do is listen.* If we clarify and ask questions-- even paraphrasing what we hear like a Rogerian therapist--it is often what our students need. Some feel ambushed by their parents, are afraid of consequences, or don't know where else to go because they spend immense time in school and are around their teachers for hours upon hours. It is when these lasting relationships become a central part of their lives and students seek us out to be the guidance that they are yearning for, that teachers who are #1 in our students' lives create relationships with students that will last a lifetime indeed.

Margot needed someone to listen to her, but it didn't stop there.

Teachers Who Understand (through Identification)

Mrs. Williams reflected on her end-of-day conversation with Margot. She was in new territory for her and did not know what to do. She knew that she could listen to Margot and help her in any way possible, but she had no connection to the subject, whatsoever. Mrs. Williams didn't have many LGBTQ friends, though she did not feel that she discriminated against LGBTQ people. She also did not have any family members or many people she even knew of who were transgender.

Lastly, Mrs. Williams never had these kinds of thoughts or feelings about her own gender. She couldn't relate through any kind of personal identification. What she could do, however, was take something that she did have in common with Margot and talk with her about that.

"Margot . . . what did you mean when you said that you were getting further away from God?"

"I . . . I dunno . . . I feel like God let me down a million times and now I don't know who I am."

"Who does God think you are?" asked Mrs. Williams.

"I think he knows that I am a good person."

"Isn't that all that really matters?"

This brief conversation between Mrs. Williams and Margot furthered the discussion about Margot's identity and God. But, things didn't end there.

Teachers Who Understand (by being Flexible)

Mrs. Williams had an idea. Since Margot talked about her disappointment in God and her lack of staying with him during tough times, Mrs. Williams made Margot a deal. She would let Margot work on a project about identity and religion--something that Margot was not only struggling with, but also something in which she was interested. Mrs. Williams had no underlying intentions. She wasn't trying to dissuade Margot from doing whatever she felt was necessary in her life in order to carry out her own fulfilled identity. She wasn't trying to thwart her thoughts and feelings by using God as a pawn to do so. What makes Mrs. Williams #1 was that she was trying to create a space where Margot could thoughtfully explore what she wanted out of life. Mrs. Williams listened to her student in as non-judgemental a way as she knew how to and helped her student feel safe to explore what she was struggling with inside. This teacher had much to learn about gender identity and Margot opened Mrs Williams' mind to what she didn't know and could now explore herself as well, to help support Margot and other gender diverse students. That is the power of understanding and flexibility coming together to support the best interest of a student and that is what this chapter contends that forever remembered teachers do.

Why?

Because YOU are #1!

CHAPTER 7
BOOK STUDY
CHALLENGE

1. List a few times when you tried to understand a student.
2. What did you do that made you an "understanding" teacher?
3. In what ways did you actively listen? What were the details of any particular student's cry for help?
4. Have you ever identified with a student's situation? How?
5. List a few times when you felt that you could not possibly identify with a student's plight. What did you do?
6. What are some ways that you could demonstrate flexibility for your students if they come to you with a problem? What do you feel that you are responsible for as their teacher?

"Yesterday I was clever, so I wanted to change the world. Today I am wise, so I am changing myself."

RUMI

Chapter 8

Because Teachers have Wisdom

Wise teachers were important to our survey respondents with an approval rating of 25.8%.

This one surprised us. While we know that wisdom is important, little did we know that having wisdom and sharing wisdom would be a memorable characteristic of teachers. If you notice, this approval rating is higher than some of the other chapters that have been previously discussed.

If one were to ask you to name people who have wisdom, you might list some of these greatest people on earth: Plato, Aristotle, Gandhi, Abraham Lincoln, Mother Theresa, Nelson Mandella, etc. Why is it that they are so revered? What is it about them that makes them stand out in our minds as "wise"?

When asking a six-year-old to name people who are wise, he responded with Pappa (his grandfather) and also his teacher. When asked why he thought they were wise, it was because, "They are smart." Being smart is much different from wisdom. Read this brief story:

She was innovative. It was the 80's but we did projects, sat in groups, some lessons were on the floor in a gathering space rather than at our desks all day. Some learning was hands-on and we had a choice in what we learned or created.

There is great wisdom in knowing what effective teaching is and isn't. It takes teachers years to build a bank of strategies and have the wisdom necessary to implement what has been learned. Being "smart" might mean that a teacher read all of the required readings for their college coursework on becoming a teacher, receiving high grades on assignments, etc.. But, wisdom has more to do with the intersection of learning and then doing something that carries out what was learned-- to know how to more effectively implement and adjust, when necessary.

In the Beginning

It is amazing to think that the concept of wisdom has long been revered by humanity. Wise people can care, be nice and become involved, but they also think outside the box to make learning happen for the individuals in their classes, and they are smart enough not to follow the grain of usual results. According to Meeks and Jeste (2009), we can learn more about the role of wisdom and how it factors in to memory as we define it here for our readers:

> Wisdom is a unique psychological trait noted since antiquity, long discussed in humanities disciplines, recently operationalized by psychology and sociology researchers, but largely unexamined in psychiatry or biology. Wisdom, a unique human attribute rich in history dating back to the dawn of civilization, is a newcomer to the world of empirical research. For centuries, wisdom was the sole province of religion and philosophy. A standard philosophical (in Greek, philos-sophia = lover of wisdom) definition of wisdom pertains to

judicious application of knowledge, and most religions have considered it a virtue. Wisdom is thought to be a complex construct, with several subcomponents.

In addition, according to the Stanford Encyclopedia of Philosophy (2017), Plato was "one of the most dazzling writers in the Western literary tradition and one of the most penetrating, wide-ranging, and influential authors in the history of philosophy." He took political movements and asked questions that were so mind-blowing and provocative that he had people from all over wanting to read or hear his every word. He had the ability to connect with them on a level that was new, exciting, innovative, and intriguing. And he is recognized as being "wise."

We can easily extrapolate this kind of epic wisdom with the teachers in our classrooms and schools, everywhere:

This teacher was the definition of above and beyond. It is not easy to create engaging lessons. It takes effort and time, but they left a lasting impression thirty years later.

The word "philosophia" means the "lover of wisdom" in Greek. People have revered intelligence, the open mind, and the willingness to be engaging when sharing their knowledge with others. Having wisdom sparks the neural pathways in the brain to help students learn new material and think in different ways. Wise teachers are the #1 teachers to many of their students. Equally unwise teachers can also be #1, but for very different reasons:

I had an Algebra teacher that was so lazy he always told us to look at previous pages in the book if we had a question. This started from day #1 of the course! I remember having straight A's and one F on my report card. When I tried to talk with him and say that I am not dumb, he said, 'Maybe you are dumb in math.'

It is difficult to fathom a teacher saying to a student that "maybe they are dumb," but there were many stories such as this from the people who were surveyed. Here, egotistical wisdom intersects with meanness, so we do not contend that wisdom can stand alone for a teacher to, forever, be remembered.

Over the Decades

Over time, scientists and researchers have started to look deeper at the importance that wisdom plays on the human brain: "Although the initial western theories of wisdom focused on cognitive abilities, there are some who drew attention to the importance of emotional self-regulation" (Meeks & Jeste, 2009).

There has been a significant amount of research done on the social-emotional health of students and teachers. Those who study wisdom and the brain are finding that there is a connection between wisdom and social-emotional health, as well as the correlation between wisdom and the ability to self-regulate behaviors.

Typically when speaking about "wise" people, we automatically think of adults. Why? Walk into any elementary classroom and you will find students who have a hard time regulating their behavior. Although this could be caused by several outside stimulants, the fact that their brain has not fully developed impacts their ability to self-regulate, and as a result, causes the inappropriate behaviors.

There are other elementary-aged students who do not have a problem with self-regulation. They tend to have an easier time sitting in class, listening dutifully to the teacher, and doing what is asked of them. They are able to think abstractly and ask questions that make others think. Ultimately, they demonstrate traits similar to those of "wise" adults. Why is that? What can educators do to help those who may struggle or those who are "wise beyond their years?"

According to Dean (2020) who researches the development of morality and wisdom in children, children who demonstrate wisdom, as well as the ability to regulate their own behaviors, "have rich and loving social networks with lots of playmates and caring adults."

Dr. Cameron Thomas may agree. In an interview with Dr. Cameron Thomas, Ward (2017) stated that, "Understanding neuroscience helps us to understand that parenting (or in our case teaching) literally builds brain networks and perception is not a direct transmission: the brain creates our perception of, and our experience of, reality."

Giving students the opportunity to socialize and learn in an environment where they know they are safe and cared about sparks the neural pathways in students' brains, ultimately making it possible for these students to gain wisdom. How *wise* is it for a teacher to know this? Below, notice how wisdom is misconstrued. There is a difference between knowing subject area content and having the wisdom to know what good teaching looks like:

He was a high school math teacher. He never actually taught anything. He did problems on the board while saying nothing and got mad if you dared ask a question. He would get so mad he would kick the metal trash can and leave the room for the rest of class.

A teacher whose students do not see them as wise, smart, caring, nice, understanding, or approachable is the teacher who does not hold the wisdom to know how to interact with all of these behavioral attributes. Imagine being a student in this teacher's math class. This teacher will, forever, be ingrained in this person's mind as a #1 teacher--but, a #1 **bad** teacher.

Wisdom can also beset the ideals of going above and beyond in one's craft and knowing how to navigate newly learned information or new-found experiences of life: "One of the most consistent subcomponents of wisdom, from both ancient and modern literature, is the promotion of common good and rising above self-interests, i.e. exhibiting prosocial attitudes and behaviors such as empathy, social cooperation, and altruism" (Meeks & Jeste, 2009). These are the teachers who go above and beyond. They "get" their students and are able to relate to them in a way that creates an exciting learning environment. These teachers are wise because they know how to connect with their students and because of this, they will always be remembered as a #1 teacher--a #1 *best* teacher.

Into the Future

Silly it sounds, but this book is, hopefully, providing some wisdom for our readers and helping others to see the power behind why we remember our teachers, forever. While it does not seem to be a highly intricate topic and actually is very basic, yet important, we feel, the role of neuroscience is a frontier worth reading about because it takes what we know by observation and adds a new element to it.

Sure, we can spot a terrible teacher from afar, but to actually know why we remember these people and why we remember the GREAT people is far more interesting in the eyes of those who seek wisdom:

> Research on the frontiers of neuroscience is radically reshaping how we understand the brain and the mind, and changing what we know about learning, memory, social behavior, parenting, decision making, trauma, and our sense of identity. This new information has direct and practical applications for teachers, therapists, nurses, social workers, mediators, life-coaches, HR professionals -indeed, all of the 'helping professions.' (Ward, 2017)

> *My high school English/Journalism teacher was very serious about her job which I respected... She treated our journalism class like it was our job and expected perfection.*

Imagine this for a future: Teachers show up when the bell rings and leave as soon as they have put in their contractual minutes at the end of the day. They teach content only out of textbooks and do not try to make learning exciting or fun for the students. Teachers teach to ensure students can answer the questions for the high-stakes standardized test because they are hoping to be compensated. They literally countdown the days and celebrate until they have vacation and not be in school teaching, not realizing that vacation is terrifying for some of the students in their class. Unfortunately, some go into the profession for weekends, summers, and the occasional snow day off.

Or, imagine this for a future: Teachers are wise and share their wisdom with their students. They teach the content in exciting ways that drive the students not only to be fully engaged, but craving to know more. Teachers create a safe environment where students choose how to learn. Students take chances, share opinions and dreams, and then develop action plans on how to make those dreams a reality regardless if they are in kindergarten or in college. They are open-minded and willing to demonstrate mistakes just so their students can see how to overcome mistakes and obstacles. Teachers have a classroom where they allow for debates so the students can learn how to articulate their opinion in a respectful manner--a place where all voices are heard and respected.

Is this a future reality? Yes. This is happening in schools and classrooms all over the country right now. But this is not the case for every school nor is it the case with all teachers. Imagine where our students would be if this was the reality for each and every one of them.

THIS is the future and school in which we want to work. These are the teachers you want to surround yourself with at all times. These are the people who are going to make you strive to be the wise educator that you have always been wanting to be for your students.

Why?

Because YOU are #1!

CHAPTER 8
BOOK STUDY
CHALLENGE

1. As educators we are always learning. Share what you are learning with your students. What are their reactions? What questions did they ask of you about your new learning? Notice to see if they are the same questions that you ask them. Why do you think that is?
2. How are you going to implement your new learning?
3. Identify how you are going to work with others to make this new learning a reality.
4. What areas will make you a better teacher--a wiser teacher?
5. What can you share with your colleagues to help them become better teachers?

"We must accept human error as inevitable - and design around that fact."

DONALD BERWICK

Chapter 9

Because Teachers are Human

Humanistic teachers were important to our survey respondents with an approval rating of 30.8%.

But, what does this chapter really get at? What we've found through our research is that teachers who show their human side--their blood, sweat, tears, victories, defeats, struggles, challenges, and everything about their lives that can create teachable moments--you know, the authentic experiences that teach us about life and tug at the heart strings of their students which can help them in ways beyond our imagination. That's what being **humanistic** means.

Teachers who try to depict a perfect life were the teachers who had terrible approval ratings. Teachers who were able to teach their students when they were down had higher approval rates. However, teachers who shared their grim stories or talked about their own problems without having any invitation to do so or without any context for helping a student were viewed as terrible teachers.

Let us explain further. Consider the story of Ms. Owens:

Ms. Owens taught seniors and had two children of her own when she was young. She struggled to find a job and had to go on public assistance. She was able to reunite with her biological father after he left Ms. Owens when she was a child and from there, she learned the harsh truths of the world and why her father left when she was in diapers. All of these experiences shaped Ms. Owens into the teacher that she is today. In fact, Ms. Owens became a teacher because her 11th grade English teacher saw the talent that she had in her writing before dropping out of school. Ms. Owens learned about her father's drug and alcohol addiction and how he became sober and clean ten years after leaving.

Ms. Owens and her father have a wonderful, loving relationship to this day which is built on their past experiences and how they both grew into the terrific people that they are today. Ms. Owens knows how her own students struggle with life and when they come to her for help and guidance, they appreciate Ms. Owens opening up.

In our chapter about the role of understanding our students, one does not have to have the same experiences in order to understand, nor does Ms. Owens have the experiences that some of her students are going through. What it does do, however, is help shine a light on teachers as struggling humans in the plight of the world and garners an appreciation from others when they hear the survival stories from our teacher mentors.

But understanding and sharing humanistic traits is only used when the time is right. Unsolicited sharing of feelings or terrible experiences can just as easily turn off students and upset them to the point where we must reflect on the damage that we do, not the help that we intend to give.

Consider the story of Mrs. Shelby as the complete antithesis to this chapter's ideals:

Mrs. Shelby went into teaching after her divorce. She would often tell her students each morning how her husband used to beat her on a daily basis after he had been drinking. She painted pictures of her home life nightmares and her students not only felt uncomfortable with Mrs. Shelby, but they thought that she was kind of crazy for telling them such personal things that were highly upsetting. From sharing that her husband used to push her down the stairs to torturing her children in front of her, Mrs. Shelby's good intentions actually backfired and turned off her students. There was no context and no playing field invitation to seek help from Mrs. Shelby and ask her for guidance or wisdom. Instead, nightmares were placed as burdens on Mrs. Shelby's students and for that reason, she was viewed as a terrible (and frightening) teacher.

When the time is right and when the context is appropriate? There were three areas that our survey respondents noted as areas of importance that define a teacher's humanistic influence on them in a positive (and contextualized) way: 1. Experiences illustrating past loss, 2. Past mistakes made and, 3. Being hurt by others in the past. We will briefly explain each one.

Teachers Who Have Experienced Loss

Loss can encompass a wide range of humanistic experiences and features that our students can learn from as we gain an inherent wisdom to be able to speak humanistically about such difficult topics. From what we might think is a minor loss, such as the loss of a cat, dog, or a parakeet, might actually rock a student's world and upset them to no end. But loss (including damage) can include a wide range of examples, and we list as many of them that we can think of without heading to any type of formal research about grief and loss. See if you can relate to the loss of any of these things below:

One might experience a loss of:

- Relatives
- Partners
- Friends
- Pets
- Lifestyle
- Income

- Health
- Mental well-being or capacity
- Food
- Clothing
- Housing
- Drive or ambition
- Happiness
- Job/occupation
- Freedom/rights
- Status
- Reputation
- Self-esteem
- Courage
- Opportunity

We are sure that there are many other types of losses, but these appeared as thematic strands among our research and connection to educators who have helped others, humanistically, to weather the storm of life-losses.

Being able to speak from a platform of humanistic experiences related to loss will set up a potential understanding through wisdom gained due to those humanistic loss experiences. But there are also mistakes that make teachers humanistic and relatable to their students. We go on to explain these in the next section.

Teachers Who Have Made Mistakes

There are degrees of mistakes and the impact on a life that exists from making a particular mistake. We contend that mistakes are natural and the degrees of mistakes can either make or break a person. Teachers who are identified as the #1 best teachers are able to rise above their own mistakes, make adjustments to their lives, and live on with a new wisdom of mistake making and rebirth. They lend stories to their students that identify with mistake making.

As stated, there are degrees of mistakes on a continuum of their relevance to experiencing a loss of some kind as the result of a mistake OR a form of hurt that we will discuss shortly. All in all, mistakes can be categorized in two different categories that we set up in order to explain this section. They are:

Conscious mistakes: Mistakes made that were purposeful.
Unconscious mistakes: Mistakes made that do not fully realize the underlying implications OR mistakes that are influenced by our inability to make a proper judgment.

A conscious mistake might be to purposefully steal from someone or cheat others out of something. Unconscious mistakes might be making an uninformed decision about how to invest money and then suffer a loss of that money due to a mistake that was inadvertently made.

Teachers Who Have Hurt Others or Who Have Been Hurt By Others

Being "hurt" does not show weakness; in fact, we contend that it demonstrates a certain kind of strength. When we talk about "hurt" and when we look at the research that acts as a foundation for this book, "hurt" was only characterized by something in which a person does to another person, emotionally. We will not address some literal types of hurt, such as being "hurt" in a car crash or being "hurt" suffered while playing football. Instead, below are categories of people who are most likely to be hurt by someone or hurt you in your life at some point:

- Spouse/significant other

- Relative
- Friend
- Acquaintance
- Person who has some sort of positional power role in your life (e.g., teacher, doctor, police officer).
- Adversary--either known or a stranger

Often, hurt has to do with conflict, controversy, or disagreement. When we experience hurt or have hurt someone in our life, emotionally or physically, we learn from those experiences and it humanizes us in the face of our students. When we experience hurt or realize how they have hurt someone else, we make a connection to our students based on our own lived experiences. As we share our lives in intricate ways, but only when an opportunity or invitation to contextually share our human side with our students exists, we can connect as teacher and student and then offer them the support that they will remember for a lifetime.

Why?

Because YOU are #1!

CHAPTER 9
BOOK STUDY
CHALLENGE

1. What are some losses that you have suffered in your life?

2. How could you help a student by sharing your own losses?

3. What are some mistakes that you have made in life?

4. How could you help a student through the lens of your own mistakes?

5. In what ways have you hurt or been hurt by others?

6. How could you help a student navigate the impact of hurting someone else or being hurt by someone else?

"True strength lies in submission which permits one to dedicate his life, through devotion, to something beyond himself."

HENRY MILLER

Chapter 10

Because Teachers are Devoted to the Profession

Devoted teachers were important to our survey respondents with an approval rating of 32%.

There is no doubt that teaching is an exceptionally challenging and demanding job. State and federal regulations placed on school districts have increased the workload and expectations for teachers (Mackenzie, Morrell, & Cook, 2004). State and federal regulations are being placed on school districts and have increased the workload and expectations for P-12 teachers (Mackenzie et al., 2004).

But yet, they still showed up to their classrooms every single day and who knows what kind of national or world crisis is going to happen in six months? Six years? Teachers have learned to be prepared with anything on any given day. Add a global pandemic from 2020 and the entire world of education as we all knew it had completely halted and shifted literally overnight and possibly forever. Among the ever changing health expectations set by the Centers for Disease Control (CDC) as well as federal and state departments of education around the United States, teachers needed to have different types of plans on any given day because they never knew when their current style of teaching was going to be changed. Teachers felt underpaid, overstressed, and worried about their students, colleagues, families and themselves.

Teachers were heroes who showed up every day because they love what they do. They love their students and they care about the education that they can provide, in whatever format that may be. Here is not only a depiction of memory, but a replication of the teacher that a student wants to become because of a teacher they had:

> *I never thought I was smart until I had an amazing English teacher in 11th grade. I was in honors English and he pushed us to always think outside the box. He told me I was a good writer. He told me I'd make a great teacher. He built me back up. I wound up student-teaching with him. I will always be thankful for him.*

Go back to the day that you decided you were going to become an educator. Why did you choose this profession? Did you choose it for the endless hours of planning and correcting, meetings that seemed to never end, or an angry parent complaining about a grade you assigned disqualifying their child from playing soccer? We can absolutely guarantee that you did not go into the profession because it was a monetarily lucrative job.

Chances are, if you were to ask most of the educators in the field, they would tell you that they love learning, they love teaching, and they love students. They love working with the minds of the students and watching them grow. Knowing the fact that they have a direct impact on the mind and life of each and every one of their students drives them to work every day. They love knowing that they actually have the ability to make the world a better place, one student at a time. "Love what you do and you will never work a day in your life," is the motto of these educators.

When one chooses their profession and honestly loves their job, they laugh, smile, and spread joy to all those around them. All of the "happy hormones" and neurotransmitters are released from the brain into the body. Dopamine is an important part of your brain's reward system. Serotonin, which helps regulate your mood as well as your sleep, appetite, digestion, learning ability, and memory. Endorphins, the body's natural pain reliever, which your body produces in response to stress or discomfort, and will increase when you engage in reward-producing activities (Raypole, 2019). Those who love teaching know that they are being rewarded by how their students turn out and what they become:

I had two teachers in high school who loved what they did and their enthusiasm was infectious. They both made me feel smart and capable every day. I ended up getting a master's degree in education because of those teachers.

There are times, unfortunately, when this love of the profession starts to dwindle. That spark that once ignited that person fades, and some become dark and they almost come to resent the work. They are soured by negative forces and in some cases are bullied by other teachers to the point where the really good teachers--the ones we want to stay in the field of education--unfortunately leave the profession.

What can be done to help keep these great teachers in the classrooms, schools, and profession? There are some areas that educators and administrators can focus on to keep their schools full of #1 great teachers: Induction Programs, Professional Development, and Teacher Leadership.

Induction Programs

The induction process is how a teacher is supported in a school and/or the education profession while in the early years of his/her career.

"Effective schools and teachers, likewise, have an induction program for all newly hired teachers," (Wong, 2002).

What these programs look like vary from district to district and even within schools of the same district. Studies have demonstrated, however, that the more structured an induction program is, the better prepared the new teachers are and the likelihood of them staying in the profession *increases.*

Picture these two scenarios:

Brand new teacher coming into the building for the first time:
"I can't wait to see my new classroom, start my new bulletin boards (that I'm going to change daily), get my class list, start planning with my PLC, learning with my colleagues…"

Mentor Teacher:
"I'm assigned to be your mentor. Bathrooms are down the hall to the right. If you need anything, you can find me in my classroom – it's usually closed so just knock on the door and come in. Or you can go see the secretary, she can help too. Oh, and don't go overboard with the bulletin boards – WE don't do that here."

Brand new teacher attending the first staff meeting:
"I don't mind being on that committee, it will help me get to know the kids and parents better. When is the PTO meeting?"

Mentor Teacher:
"Don't volunteer – we don't get paid to do volunteer work. That includes PTO meetings. It's outside of the contract."

--Or scenario #2--

Brand new teacher coming into the building for the first time:

"I can't wait to see my new classroom, start my new bulletin boards (that I'm going to change daily), get my class list, start planning with my PLC, learning with my colleagues…"

Mentor A Teacher:
"Let me show you around the school and get you acquainted with the building. I know that you will have the opportunity to meet the whole staff later but I'd like to introduce you to our PLC. We are a great team who get together at least twice a week: once to plan together and the other to go over student data. I can't wait to see your bulletin boards. They are not my strong point, but the kids love them. Maybe you can give me some ideas!"

Brand new teacher attending the first staff meeting:
"I don't mind being on that committee, it will help me get to know the kids and parents better. When is the PTO meeting?"

Mentor B Teacher:
"I know it may seem like extra work, but working on some of these committees gives us the opportunity to work with others outside our PLC. It also helps when we attend the PTO meetings. You get a great feel of who the parents are and it's a great opportunity to share the great things going on in your class. We can go over all of this information when we meet at our weekly meeting. Remember, if you need anything, I am literally the next door down. Just walk on in!"

In these two scenarios, which new teacher is more likely to keep their love of education? Which one is going to feel supported and know that they have a team working with them on behalf of all of the students?

On the contrary, which new teacher is likely to get a bad taste in their mouth if they do not comply?

Professional Development

Learning to become effective educators comes from the training received in schools both prior to and during their educational careers. The concept of professional development is interesting if we approach it like we do as teachers to students. Not all professional development/lessons meet the needs of all teachers/students. The professional development needs to be personalized to the individual teacher. One of the most powerful ways that professional development can be offered at little to no cost is if teachers teach each other.

If an administrator has created an environment where teachers teach or share their knowledge with each other during a staff meeting, the likelihood of those learning increases dramatically than if they are receiving canned training. They are more invested in the learning and are more likely to then implement their new learning, or if they have questions about the new learning, they are comfortable going to their colleague and asking for clarification.

If you are able to hold staff meetings in classrooms, this gives the rest of the staff the opportunity to see their colleagues' spaces, ask questions, and learn from those classroom teachers. This is especially eye-opening if you have an elementary school where a fifth grade teacher has to sit in a kindergarten chair! What an incredible perspective!

Ultimately, if a district truly appreciates and respects its teachers, they will offer professional development that meets the needs of the teachers. The more a district invests in a teacher, the less likely the teacher is to lose that love of teaching and then leave the school and/or the profession.

> *She always made me feel I was loved and cared about as a person. I had her as a teacher forty-nine years ago and we still are in touch, getting together about every six months for dinner. I am now a teacher because of her and she gives me great teaching advice.*

Teacher Leadership

Teacher leadership is a necessary part of a highly successful school. According to the Association of Curriculum Development and Supervision (ASCD, 2014),

> The defined position of "teacher leader" is, increasingly, serving as a cornerstone of a well-functioning school system, especially given the ever-evolving demands of the education profession, such as more rigorous standards, high-stakes federal and state achievement mandates, increasingly diverse student populations, greater numbers of school-aged children living in poverty, and the hyper pace of technological change. (7).

Leadership opportunities for teachers come in many different forms: the official stipend position of a teacher who serves as the conduit between the staff and administration, the position that was elected or chosen to serve in that capacity either for a department or pod, someone who takes over the building when the principal is out, or a person who steps up and takes the opportunity to lead a professional development offering for their peers.

I was given extra responsibilities, not just extra work, because I was the top student in my class.

People strive to be the best they can be and when given the opportunity to shine, in an environment that allows them to make mistakes and it is seen as growth, this will happen. This is leadership. This is keeping those "happy hormones" flowing through the body and that love of the profession an eternal flame.

Creating a culture within a school where a teacher is completely involved, part of a collaborative team, feels fully supported, and is given opportunities to stretch into leadership roles are all a part of keeping that love of teaching alive in many educators. Keeping these teachers who honestly LOVE teaching, and these will be the teachers who are #1 for their students.

Answer this question honestly to yourself: "Why do you still love teaching?" If that spark has started to fade, what can you do to reignite that flame and rejuvenate yourself and others around you? Why would you want to do this? Why do you want the reason when you walk into a classroom for every student to look at you and smile because they know they are going to have a great day with you?

Why?

Because YOU are #1!

CHAPTER 10 BOOK STUDY CHALLENGE

1. Consider the three topics that were shared in this chapter: teacher induction programs, professional development, and teacher leadership. Which of these three areas could you learn more about and then implement one thing that can improve any of these areas?

2. Create an action plan on how you can implement this strategy. If you do this, you will not only ignite your flame, but you may add fuel to someone else's as well.

"The marble not yet carved can hold the form of every thought the greatest artist has."

MICHELANGELO

Conclusion
Etched in Our Minds, Forever, Good and Bad

As we examined both positive and negative memories from our survey respondents, it is interesting to finish with data about negative memories, but illustrate a positive story that we hope will last with you for a lifetime. Look at these statistics from our research which survey respondents cited as part of the negative flurry of memories that lasted with them to this day:

Memories of uncaring teachers = 49.2%
Memories of mean teachers = 66.1%
Memories of teachers who had no sense of humor = 18%
Memories of boring teachers = 23%
Memories of uninvolved teachers = 16.4%
Memories of teachers who were poorly acclimated to life = 5.5%
Memories of self-absorbed teachers = 23.5%
Memories of teachers who gave up (or were quitters) about something major in their life = 6%
Memories of teachers who did not choose teaching as their primary devoted profession = 10.9%

There were other reasons why teachers had negative impacts on our survey respondents which totaled an additional 35%, but these ranged from absolutely tragic memories (e.g., abuse) to nit-picky reasons (e.g., didn't like how they were graded). We didn't include every one of these subcategories because the overall research showed high correlations only to the areas that we outlined for you in this book.

With that said, we think it is only appropriate to end on a high note.

Now, meet Mrs. Malcolm!

Mrs. Malcolm wore a red cape while her 3rd graders entered the classroom with ecstatic, energized surprise. On her face, she wore a shiny, silver mask with an incredible series of bling jewels which, Danica, one of her students, thought were real diamonds:

"Mrs. Malcolm, how much did you actually **PAY** for that mask?"

"Oh, silly . . . $.50 for the whole thing," Mrs. Malcolm responded while spinning in her cape with a 360 degree twirl.

Mrs. Malcolm began to shout about how the "Redcoats" were coming as if she were a modern day Paul Revere with no horse, but a purse that she opened containing Sour Patch Kids candy packets! Holding a red piece up in the air, she threw it up and caught it in her mouth just before it landed on the mask that she briskly pulled back.

But then . . .

Mrs. Malcolm pretended to choke!

With a dramatic gasp and a cough, her face smiled, with her mask pulled back, and her left eye winked at her class (so she was able to non-verbally tell her 3rd graders that she wasn't *really* choking after all).

She asked her class a question while pretending-choking . . .

"What if . . . just what if . . . Paul Revere was not heard . . . *couldn't* be heard because he was choking on a piece of candy while riding into town? What would happen, children? Just WHAT would have happened on that day in history . . . a day that would have possibly changed our world forever?" Mrs. Malcolm dramaticized.

The class went wild; they laughed until they cried and then they laughed again wondering how to answer Mrs. Malcolm's question.

In one particular class in one particular small elementary school in one particular city in one particular state in one particular country on this planet . . . Mrs. Malcolm would be remembered, forever, by her students.

We end with the story of Mrs. Malcolm because she will, forever, be remembered as a #1 teacher for what, we guess, so many of her students (even when they graduate, grow up, get married, get a new job, have children of their own, etc.) will remember because Mrs. Malcolm was a part of their schooling and their lives as someone who influenced them the most. Mrs. Malcolm didn't TRY to have her students like her. That just came with the territory. What she was, though, was a teacher who cared for her students, was nice to them, funny, exciting (cape and all), involved, understanding, wise, humanistic, and devoted to her career.

Danica will not remember much about her 3rd grade curriculum. Most of us don't. But, Danica will always remember the red cape, the Sour Patch Kids and so much more about Mrs. Malcolm . . .

Why?

Because she is #1

And . . .

You can be #1 too!

"Memory is the diary that we all carry about with us."

OSCAR WILDE

Appendices

We offered our survey respondents an opportunity to share a positive or negative narrative about their teachers' memories if they chose to do so. Below, you will find a small collection of responses from some of our respondents who decided to participate in this additional activity. Enjoy!

Note: Text was captured as it was originally submitted, so typos, grammatical errors, etc. may be found.

Appendix A: Negative Narratives Shared by Survey Respondents

I went to an all girls High School, in my junior year the history teacher walked into class and said the following,"Let's face it girls, none of you are going to be brain surgeons or marry rich husbands. You all just need to enroll in secretarial school so that you can make money. None of you should waste money applying to college."

Teacher said, "Well that's why we have people who work at McDonalds and why we have people who are CEO's."

Gym teacher was a bully.

Many stories but basically it was the affect. The teacher was never smiling and was more about compliance and work completion than celebrating the educational journey.

They said to the class, "This is my last year. I don't care."

When I expressed concern about this teacher he asked to see me after school and while I was sitting at the desk, he moved in very close, was above me, invaded my personal space, and while under the guise of "communicating" with me, made it clear he was "above" me, both literally and figuratively. He didn't sit next to me. He lorded over me. This is only ONE story from this man. He was a huge influence on me as a teacher of what NOT to do, so at least there's that. Looking back, I didn't have the words to express what he was doing (I just felt intimidated on a subconscious level), but now I know he knew EXACTLY what he was doing. I'm sure I wasn't the only one.

They called me stupid. They chose to believe I was lazy rather than provide me strategies to help with my disability- which was not understood back then.

Each day we walked into seeing six chalkboards of handwritten notes of history content we spent the hour copying. No conversation. He sat at desk and we would just copy what was on the board. Everyday until the test. Then repeat for the next until. All year long.

I was just a number.

I had a history teacher who thought she knew everything and discouraged anyone from asking probing questions or challenging an idea.

Physiology teacher put me in a trash can once.

He was just sarcastic beyond imagination, and poked fun at students in class more than he taught.

I had an ag teacher in high school who gave us a book and would either sit at his desk or leave the room. I was really excited about the class because I was interested in livestock and veterinary science so it was a huge disappointment. It stifled my interest.

He was my Geometry teacher. Instead of teaching Geometry he showed us magic tricks from his side job. Now every time that I wish I understood Geometry Theories I am reminded of this teacher.

During music class in MS, I was told to lip sync instead of singing because I was off-key. She never taught me HOW to sing correctly and to this day, I don't sing in public (nor do I know how to "carry a tune.")

During 9th grade math, I was bored because I was advanced and knew much of the material already. I tried asking questions about patterns I noticed and my teacher told me (in front of my parents at conferences) to stop asking so many questions because I was just confusing my classmates.

In first grade, I was bored during reading (because I was already reading at a 5th grade reading level) and so I would talk to my peers in class. My teacher sat me in the corner by myself so I couldn't (talk to anyone) until my mom came in and complained about her policy of isolating me in the back of class.

In sophomore year of high school, my religion teacher told me it was impossible for a husband to rape his wife. I decided if that's what Catholicism taught, I didn't want to be Catholic anymore.

My teachers in my college classes stated, "We feel that you will fail if you were to try student teaching." This is despite doing everything that was asked of me during practicums and classes. It was only after having to jump through multiple hoops that I realized that it wasn't about my ability to teach, but about their ability to guide me in becoming a teacher.

My high school Spanish teacher questioned why I was in her 4th year spanish class after receiving A's and B's throughout the previous 3 years.

A pregnant classmate of mine had been raising her hand for minutes while this professor continuously wrote on a blackboard with her back to us all. Finally turning around the professor called on this classmate who asked for clarification because she was "lost." This professor rolled her eyes, looked straight at this classmate and sternly said, "Find yourself." Turned back around and continued her racehorse show.

My grade four teacher was extremely boring. I hated the whole year.

She told my parents I couldn't read and she didn't think I belonged in 1st grade. What she refused to acknowledge was the fact that I had been reading for 2-3 years and could not be bothered to challenge me.

The teacher did not build a relationship nor connect to me when I was struggling in Algebra II. She was more worried about teaching the content than teaching kids.

She would slap and hit me when I did not get my math problems right and I did NOT go to a Catholic school!

Always putting you down and being compared to the more fortunate student. "You'll never be as successful as …"

She put me down. She did not name me, but made sure I knew she was talking about me. She said my paper was one of the reasons she was retiring. I was kind, quiet, and tried. I did not care about the subject and she did not go out of her way to try to make it better. She was retiring so she did not care. That did not make her any less nasty.

He insisted the text of the Foundation in Education class was THE authority on the history of education and did not allow for discussion that drew on other sources.

She clearly had class favorites and those who she would use as negative examples to the rest of the class.

The priority was covering the curriculum. It was mere mention and no depth.

My sixth grade teacher made fun of kids all the time. For example, she used to stutter to make fun of a girl who stuttered. She also whipped erasers at kids' heads. She told me I was dumb and when she asked the class—who wanted to be in honors classes in middle school, I raised my hand and she stopped class to burst out laughing at me. I still lack confidence in many areas of my life but I've been a teacher for 22 years and she taught me what not to do. She knocked so many kids down.

When mentioning I wanted to go to college, I was told to "just"go to community college because I would only end up married with children. I think part of it was because my mom was a secretary; my dad was a high school dropout truck driver.

He was the principal of the high school I attended. He taught Algebra 1 my Freshman year. I was a tuition student from a different town and he made it clear he did not think any of "us" should be in that school. He would not give me any extra help. I had to get help from the other students. I got three D's and a C in the class. I was an A-B student who graduated 3rd in my class in the 8th grade.

I had an Algebra teacher that was so lazy he always told us to look at previous pages in the book if we had a question. This started from day 1 of the course! I remember having straight A's and one F on my report card. When I tried to talk with him and say that I am not dumb, he said, "Maybe you are dumb in math." He had a failure rate that was unacceptable.

Yelled and turned over a girl's desk because it was messy

My journalism teacher in high school only wanted to be a dean. He had to be a teacher first before getting an administrative position. He did not focus on teaching and his final exam had nothing to do with class as if the class did not matter. He also told me not to pursue writing or journalism. Despite his ignorance, I still pursued my goal and earned my BA in journalism, 2 master degrees, became a writer for the local paper, and wrote four books.

She hated me because I passed all of her super easy tests without doing any of the homework or class notes. She was angry because I was smart and did not follow her pointless rules.

He was a teacher who appeared to seek approval from the jocks and cheerleaders in school; he told jokes that were not funny or were borderline inappropriate; he wasted class time- almost like he expected us to teach ourselves Geometry (I had to get a tutor)- so he could talk about what was going on in sports, or in the personal lives of SOME students (who is going with whom to the dances, who is dating whom, who went where and did what over the weekend)- looking for gossip, or creating it. This was a male teacher, by the way, in his late 30's or early 40's. He also sold insurance as a side job--and was constantly giving out his cards to students to give to parents--or asking if they needed insurance of some kind. I do not know what kind(s) of insurance he sold. His lack of teaching ability became a striking contrast during my high school career when an award winning, fabulous, recognized, truly dedicated teacher in this same building was tragically killed in a motorcycle accident over spring break one year--such a shock. Adolescents being who we were- made horrible comments about the real tragedy being the bad teacher(s) left to teach. This geometry teacher was not respected by students, and I would venture not by staff either. Even the jocks and cheerleaders who appeared to be his favorites did not respect him. Sad.

I was so scared of my second grade teacher that I often threw up and had hives on my arms. I still cringe when I think about her.

She just screamed all the time.

I was sent to the office for asking a legitimate question, "Why did we spend music class doing worksheets instead of music?" It felt very unfair.

He slammed kids up against the wall. Scary guy!

She was my 5th grade reading teacher. She was old and her breath stank. I remember that and the day she grabbed me by the face and said something that was not nice. I hated her from that day forward.

There was a lot of yelling in response to students showing disrespect to him because we genuinely did not like him. He was unable to connect and build relationships with students, undynamic teaching strategies, and seemed to not care at all if learning was accessible or interesting to students. He just sat at his desk all day long.

You could just tell she did not want to be there. It was not only one experience but rather an entire year.

The teacher told me he would block me from taking Algebra in HS and I would never amount to anything. I mailed him a copy of each advanced degree I got to prove him wrong.

One of my teachers had no classroom management skills. She got so frustrated every day that she ran out of the room crying at least three times per week. The class finished the day with the principal supervising.

She told the class she did not give F's because we were not failures. She gave G's because we were goners.

We had a class discussion about continents. I said that it looked as though all the separate continents could have been one large continent and she made a snide remark. I did not take any risks in that class again.

I remember the teacher always being mad and complaining about how things worked.

I was paddled in 5th grade for getting a 74 on a math test. It was my first day back to school after a week-long absence due to being ill. The paddling left me bruised. I will never forget it.

She was always unhappy and refused to listen. She physically hurt kids who made bad choices.

She was the only one I had who did no take the time to work with me on what I needed. She taught one way, and for those of us who didn't understand, she took things out on us personally.

In high school my algebra teacher told me that I wasn't good at math, so I would never be a doctor. Much less get into college. I finally had my grandmother (former math teacher) start tutoring me and I was finally learning and succeeding. He then accused me of cheating. Because if he could not teach me. No one could. I was a "lost cause" and so I must be cheating.

My fifth grade teacher had favorites. We lived in a poor community. She would take her favorites to DQ for ice cream as a reward. The rest of us could not ever make her happy or proud. I am a first born and loved school and was a very compliant child. It just hurt.

Teacher was shocked I would apply for scholarships my senior year since I was pregnant. I was told I should not waste my time or that of the scholarship committee. I was only going to be a welfare mom. I now have a doctorate in educational leadership.

He told me that though I understood the concepts and could do the math, I would fail for putting definitions in my own words. He said any other professor would give me an A. He made me drop my math major.

My 5th grade teacher slammed her hand on my desk and asked why I was so stupid.

He was my high school math teacher who never actually taught anything. He did problems on board while saying nothing, then got mad if you dared ask a question. He would get so mad that he would kick the metal trash can and leave the room for the rest of class.

My first education-specific class in college was health. The adjunct professor was less than stellar. She demanded a high-end product with little instruction or guidance as to how to successfully complete the work. Everyone in the class spent tons of time researching the content and writing lesson plans in a format that made no sense and was not explained. (Most of us had never even seen lesson plans at this point.) When the projects were returned one student had a passing grade-and only by one point. Obviously we were upset. She asked me how I felt about it in front of the class. I sighed and mumbled "Well, there goes my A." I had earned most of the available points up until this point. She proceeded to rip me a new one in front of the class. I was livid. She asked a question and I answered honestly. I have never been shamed for answering a question. My classmates, most of whom I did not know, consoled me after class and encouraged me to report her to the dean. I cooled off and made an appointment to see her during her limited office hours. I told her that I didn't appreciate being shamed in front of my peers for answering a question honestly and felt that she owed me a public apology. She dismissed me from her office. In the next class she said she was sorry if some of us (glancing at me) were disappointed in our performance. As soon as class was over, I went straight to the dean's office. Before we filled out our surveys at the end of the term, one of my classmates stood up and addressed the class reminding them about her treatment of me and how little we had learned that would actually help us compared to all of her other education courses. That teacher impacted all of us in a negative way. We learned a great deal about how NOT to talk to our students and the importance of scaffolding when teaching new/difficult concepts and materials.

I had a physical education teacher that was physically and verbally abusive.

They had a very boring, monotone voice.

I asked him for help with my math and he refused to help me. He told me to ask my friends.

The teacher was more interested in teaching girls how to pluck their eyebrows then English.

This particular person refused to allow female students to use the restroom unless it was "that time" and demanded this be said out loud in class.

The music teacher scared me to death. She would glare at us. And when she separated me from my best friend, I started crying and she blew over it like I was a baby--at 2nd grade.

As a senior, I was so excited to enter college as an education major. My photo journalism teacher spoke so poorly of the profession and how impossible it was becoming, I actually changed my major. Luckily, I changed it back the spring semester of my freshman year.

I don't remember my junior year English teacher caring whether we learned or not.

I had an elementary teacher who ignored me completely for days at a time.

After two weeks of kindergarten, I was moved to a first grade class. It was a Friday, and it was time for a spelling test. The teacher slapped a piece of paper down on the desk, and said, "If you're so smart, you can take the spelling test." I remember crying (and failing the spelling test). I don't remember anything else about first grade!

Art teacher told me I had no talent and should never take Art classes again. This was said in front of the entire class.

I remember asking if a certain mathematical problem could be solved using something else I had just learned and he dismissed me and told me to just focus on his method. This was common place and questions were not welcome.

When I would talk in class, I would get chalk thrown at me and get told to shut up.

He had a fixed mindset; believed I could not be successful in his class.

The teacher accused me of being disrespectful when I spoke to him and refused to believe that I did not say what he thought I said. He walked me to the principal's office. My first time there ever. I was in the 5th grade.

My first grade teacher only wore black, she never smiled, she was always grumpy. She left after that year.

Art teacher said I was not good enough to be an art teacher.

She dressed up as Viola Swamp and scared the crap out of me in 1st grade. The kids that had been causing trouble thought it was hysterical.

I was late to school one day because I was in a car accident. When I showed up to class she was mean and did not even care what had happened even though I was never late.

I was taking pre-calculus and the teacher made me feel stupid. My dad was an engineer and tutored me every night, but I still did poorly on the tests. When I went to have the teacher sign my drop slip, he said, "I was expecting this." He let me know that because I did not go to him for extra help, I could not possibly be learning the "right way".

It is more of the feeling. I spent every recess in the "penalty box" at recess just watching other kids play in 2nd grade because I talked too much (still made all A's).

My 3rd grade teacher made me stand at the board until I solved a long division math problem even though I had drawn a complete blank and could not remember what to do.

My teacher in the sixth grade publicly shamed me for bringing a concern about the treatment of students who were struggling. I cried to my mom and the next day the teacher publicly called me out for being a tattle tale: "Jenny's mother doesn't like the way I treat some of you. But I don't care what Jenny's mother thinks and I'm going to keep doing what I'm doing, is that okay with you, Jenny?"

She was too structured.

My 4th and later 5th grade teacher (I was lucky enough to have her twice in a row) did not like kids. She was unkind and did not know how to handle struggling students (me). I was not a bad kid, School was tough. She eventually told my parents that I would never go to college or even likely graduate from high school. I did graduate high school, went to college, taught, went back for my master's and am now an administrator.

We learned nothing. The teacher taught the basics and did nothing to make a connection with anyone. They would be upset when students did not behave and punished the entire class.

She told my mother at best I was a C student.

I was in my third year of math in high school. I could not understand Geometry. I am the youngest of seven and no one in the family had taken the course. My mom went to the classroom with me to beg for help since I was failing. The woman replied, "My hours are 8 a.m. to 3 p.m., tell her to ask a friend, I have my own life to live." I failed the class. I did not sign up for 12th grade Trigonometry. When my Senior year started, she was gone and there was no chance of me adding Math since all sections were full. So, I had a year of Ethnic Cooking and a loss of my last two years of H.S. Math. To this day, I tell my students why I will always be there when they do not understand their math. I work with them before and after school anytime needed to assure they understand their work.

The teacher told me I was stupid and lazy. I have Dyslexia and struggled. They were rude to almost everyone.

In fifth grade I had a teacher that was basically an old school marm. She was an old spinster and had no idea about the real world or had any kind of patience for kids. She was always picking on my clothes and was just mean in general. Years later I became a teacher at the very same school and I ran into her at a school function well after she had retired. She said that I was always one of her favorites, which I find difficult to believe and then told me to call her by her first name since we were colleagues now. I could not do that. She still scares me.

I was taped to my chair from my chest down to my feet.

My first teacher yelled at me and kept me from recess twice for writing the letter "s" crooked.

I had a high school teacher who could not connect with kids and a middle school teacher who whipped an eraser in the class. It happened to hit me in the mouth...embarrassing!

A male teacher that taught math was highly involved in sports, refused to help me but helped those that participated in any type of sport. He was not aware that my home life did not allow the participation of sports.

He made fun of me every day.

It was my math teacher. She would never explain why an answer was right or if you did not do it her way. She would still count it as wrong.

Teacher smacked me in the head with a music book.

The teacher took me out to the hallway and slammed my head against the door.

My phy ed teacher was mean and treated students differently.

I had a classmate with very limited resources and a very difficult home situation. Our teacher was unkind. She pointed out his clothes (limited, ill fitting, over worn), shoes that did not fit, who was often tardy (no working family vehicle), and he often did not complete homework. I cried many days thinking of my third grade classmate because he needed support, not ridicule. She retired soon after this but she should have never had the opportunity to work with this child.

A teacher called out a dress I was wearing for being way too short in front of the class. I was growing and had to do my own laundry. It had shrunk and probably did not fit me great--but doing it in front of the entire class and waiting for me to respond was so humiliating that a boy in the class told her to leave me alone.

We had a rough high school--my physiology teacher put me in a trash can once (he married a classmate that summer--probably 20 years his junior)!

I was sitting at my desk and was screamed at when I did not answer a question.

My middle-school science teacher made fun of the books I read. I was an avid reader of fantasy novels. She would pick them up off my desk, read the titles, and scoff in front of the class.

My teacher basically called me an idiot by saying I have a smooth brain.

One teacher only "engaged" students she felt were worth her attention.

He was gay and tried to "invite" me to a get together at his home. I respectfully declined and he became punitive with his grading policy toward me.

My teacher was not accommodating and only cared about their own convenience rather than student education.

My phys. ed. teacher threw balls at your head if you were not listening.

I was a mean girl..to peers and authority alike, it was what I knew and how I sought help through negative ways. When people gave up on me, I became meaner. I could name many times when I experienced a negative time with a teacher.

I was more than half way into my doc program and the professor told me I was a horrible writer and that I should drop out of the program. I dropped her class and it set me back more than a year. She was not given tenure and fired from the university. She was notorious for being abusive to grad students.

My teacher told me that I had no chance to go to a college such as Canisius.

My teacher made me feel like an idiot for answering a question wrong.

I just remember feeling like she hated me. I was in 5th grade. She was my math teacher. I had to go to her room for math- I was a poor math student. I was embarrassed and she made me feel shameful. I recall telling my mother that she hated me and they responded with, "Teachers don't hate students." Hmmmmmm...

My middle school algebra teacher told my mother that I was not good at math and probably should not take more difficult math classes in high school. Six years later, I graduated from college with a degree in math!

My teacher was mean... Just plain mean.

I had a teacher who used strong punishments for all. She provided a "same rules for everyone" classroom full of consequences that were unrelated to the action.

When I was in second grade I had an extremely strict and unforgiving teacher. She would shame students in front of the rest of the class for not having their pencil, not having work completed, and not being 100% compliant. She used fear and intimidation to keep "order" in the classroom. I was a bright student but saw the excessive busy work, especially with our spelling exercises, unnecessary and not truly beneficial to my learning, nor was I engaged as a 7 year old who would rather play than sit and write my words 10 times each, the spelling book exercises, and writing 3 sentences per word using the word in the sentence (20 words per week). At some point I decided I was not going to do the spelling anymore and refused. Initially I was sent home with a note, and was disciplined by my parents. I still refused. Then she took it to the next level and paddled me. This took place right outside of the door of the classroom where my classmates could still see. After 6 weeks of this (and getting disciplined at home, too), she took me to the principal. He paddled me once. I was tired of the paddling and finally went back to doing my spelling. To this day I dislike her.

It seemed like everyday we would get a sheet of paper or a packet and we would just take notes everyday.

My 8th grade health teacher was a pervert. His behavior today would land him in jail.

A teacher asked me to press a button on the stage to put the screen up in the auditorium because it was a band day. The teacher thought it was the day where our group was in a different room and another class was in the auditorium. The other teacher yelled "no" to me and started jumping over instruments and yelling and being so rude that all he had to do was press one button and my teacher did not back me up-- he just left.

My teacher called me out in front of the entire class that I had a wrong answer and announced it.

The instruction was terrible! Relationships with students weren't even on the radar. He only lectured and graded--that was all he cared about.

They pre-decided who the smartest kids in the class were in 9th grade and verbalized that they would be the most successful all based on what community they lived in.

The teacher dismissed me from the moment I walked into class. She did not appreciate questions, had little patience, and did nothing to engender any enthusiasm for learning. I was in third grade.

The teacher was verbally and physically abusive.

My best friend was killed by a drunk driver and my teacher spent the entire class period holding up the news article and talking about how it was her fault for walking where there were no sidewalks. I sat there crying and he never even addressed me.

My 3rd grade teacher made it very well known who she liked and who she did not. I went from never missing school to never wanting to go to school.

My English grammar teacher who red lined everything and basically killed my love of writing.

A certain Professor, from Canada, tried pushing his socialist views.

When I was in school, I was involved in all aspects of school: music, art and more.... she was not willing to let me be in art since music was taking over all that I was doing. As a result, I dropped 6th grade art and kept going with music. I became a music teacher btw.

She did not show up for a meeting after school with me to go over a quiz we had.

She did not care that I was struggling in school and felt sick. She continued to yell at me and would tell me I am stupid.

I had an art teacher in middle school who inevitably told students what was "wrong" with their artwork. Every class she would mark up my art and tell me to rework it the way she wanted; once taking a ballpoint pen to my piece. After each student met with her we would ask each other, "What was wrong today?"

He accused me of going in his grade book to change a grade in front of the entire class. I was mortified.

I had a teacher who said we would have a Play Group. We went to meetings after school for about two months. At the last minute he said we were not good enough. We stopped rehearsing, going to the meetings, everything. We had to listen to so many stories about himself. He was a big, uncaring, self-absorbed idiot.

A teacher in 7th grade gossiped about me with two students in class and openly made fun of me.

Appendix B: Positive Narratives Shared by Survey Respondents

I went to a K-8 school and the teachers all told us throughout all nine years that we had to graduate from high school and college. Had I not been in such an affirming and determined environment, the negativity of my high school teachers may have caused me to give up on myself. I have since gone on to complete my aster's degree.

They just showed how much they cared about each student and really showed how much they wanted each one of their students to succeed.

My senior English/homeroom teacher helped me become more involved in school.

My teacher was always excited about teaching (especially Science) and she always checked in with students on a personal level (asking about family, extra-curricular activities, groups, etc.)

They let us learn about life and take off on what interested us.

In addition to being kind, funny, and excited about both his subject AND his students, he NEVER failed to treat us like human beings. One of many stories involves one of the few times I cut class. I was going through an incredibly overwhelming time and I skipped the last two classes of the day (one of which was his). I had to be back on campus, though, to catch the school bus home and, upon my return, I ran into him. He asked me where I was and because I had tremendous respect for him, I told him the truth. He looked at me, said something to the effect of how he knew I must be going through some tough stuff because otherwise I would not have done something like that and then he said, "Okay. See you tomorrow." I never heard anything else about it. I tell that story not to say look at how he let me get away with something, but because he was a man of empathy, compassion, and understanding. Again, that was just ONE story of how well he treated us and how wise he was. I was a drama major and English minor and you would think that my favorite teacher would have been an English or drama teacher, but no. This man was my high school Spanish teacher. I was so incredibly fortunate to have him. To this day, thirty days into my career as a teacher, his example informs everything I do in the classroom. And when I was a sub and had to sub in Spanish classes, I stole his approach, his jokes, and even his mannerisms. :)

My teacher told me I had potential to do great things. They made me feel safe, accepted and intelligent and the classroom felt like home.

She was innovative. It was the 80s but we did projects, sat in groups. Some lessons were on the floor in a gathering space rather than at our desks all day. We had some hands-on learning experiences and we had choices.

Mr. D cared and believed in me!!

My 11th grade government teacher took an interest in challenging me and pushing me to be better.

Mrs. B read us the entire Little House Series- and now at 60- we all remember and value that.

She challenged me, and not in a "You can do better because I say so" way, but in her feedback and willingness to sit down next to you and guide you but yet never do the work for you.

My high school English/Journalism teacher was very serious about her job which I respected. I was a hard worker in class and it meant a lot to me that she valued that and took time to really look over the things we completed. She treated our journalism class like it was our job and expected perfection. She was there to do her job and do it right and I could feel it. I never felt cheated.

I was chosen by this teacher to accompany her and one other student to Washington DC after graduation.

Mr "Red" always showed he cared about you. He offered sound feedback and advice, never dwelled on our sometimes naughty behaviors. He was always looking forward. He knew the personal backgrounds of each of his students (small school/small town). He was active in every aspect of our school. He was "that teacher" which everyone loved and respected.

I had a math teacher who was funny and engaging. She encouraged my questions and told me I was ahead of the game when my observation was about something we had not discussed in class yet.

My ELA teacher spoke to us about real emotions and life through the required readings. He did not shy away from (age appropriate) conversations about love, sex or LGBTQ people.

I have, luckily, had a number of caring, supportive teachers who have greatly influenced me professionally and personally. Each one of them taught me to be passionate, involved, and willing to go the extra mile. They set clear expectations, yet were able to see when a flexible situation was needed.

When I was an elementary student I was diagnosed with a processing disability. I did not know why, but subjects like math and reading just never made sense. I thought I was dumb because no matter how hard I tried, I felt like I just could not do it. Through the determination and support of an elementary school teacher who never gave up on me, even when I wanted to, I slowly developed the skills to not only succeed in these subjects, but excel. When I got to college, reflecting on the influence this teacher had on my own education and confidence, I decided to become a teacher myself so that one day I might be able to change a student's life like this teacher did for me.

Teachers that cared about me were always positive.

They both knew I wanted to learn from them. They trusted me to work on my own and encouraged me to go into teaching.

My third grade teacher was amazing. She is the reason I decided to be a teacher. She always found something positive in each student and made learning fun. In the 70's when most teachers were teaching with a basal and worksheets, she was not. We were doing project based learning before that was even a "thing." She had the best sense of humor too and knew how to connect to each student.

My teacher encouraged me and gave me goals every day to accomplish.

My teacher never gave up on me at a time that I had put aside my schooling. He found a way to reel me back in.

You can tell the teachers that love to teach and you can tell the ones that teach because it is too late to change career paths. I had many wonderful teachers that saw struggling students and took the time to try to help! It goes a long way and it always made me want to try to do better.

I recall many gentle but firm corrections to my behavior. They provided a model for me as a teacher responding to the behavior in a constructive way without denigrating the person.

He knew his students personally and was able to find what motivated each of them to succeed.

He was the outing club advisor too. I remember him getting us all to sing "Don't Worry Be Happy" on a way back from a hike.

The professor was about preparing us to think critically. It was very challenging. He was personalized in his approach.

I never thought I was smart until I had an amazing English teacher in 11th grade. I was in honors English and he pushed us to always think outside the box. He told me I was a good writer. He told me I would make a great teacher. He built me back up. I wound up student-teaching with him. I will always be thankful to him.

She believed in me and said I was a good writer.

I was chubby and many of the kids were mean to me. My teacher always encouraged me to believe in myself and my abilities. She did not let me obsess over my weight, she made me focus on my intelligence.

My teacher apologized to me.

My English Teacher in High School was understanding of my need to learn basic life skills. He would never speak down to me. He treated me like an independent adult as opposed to treating me like a child. I was in dire need of this kind of support, it helped me to accept responsibility and to focus on the things I needed to do to get my High School diploma and begin my adult life. Prior to his influence, my mind was constantly racing in an attempt to make sense of all the things I was going through. I wanted out of my Foster Home, I wanted to be accepted by friends, I wanted good grades but could not seem to understand what was expected of me. I no doubt had a learning disability. It is very difficult to concentrate when one's mind is in a constant struggle. He was a mentor I believe and took the time to talk to me and help me make sense of all the crazy things I was going through. Something clicked within me and suddenly school work was no longer a struggle. I also had come to an agreement with the principal and other teachers that so long as I passed my test that I could come and go as I pleased so that I may maintain my job and apartment. This agreement allowed me to take care of myself and to feel respected as an adult and not just some other reckless teen. I believe to this very day that teachers need to prepare us for the future as adults.

They just cared. They talked to me about stuff other than the school.

He was excited about teaching, he got along with the students, and he did not let anyone feel left out. Even though he joked around while teaching, he still taught what needed to be taught. He always had school spirit and was not afraid to show it.

My favorite English teacher stood on his desk teaching us (way before this type of thing was made popular via social media and fancy films).

I had an extraordinary science teacher. Teaching was a second career for him- he was so dedicated and made sure each and every student was given the opportunity to master the content- phenomenal. There was a public school teacher whom I had the privilege of working with at church to teach young students (I became a special education teacher). She was a special education teacher, and we talked A LOT about helping students be ready to learn, and helping students learn in multiple ways. She was not my teacher, but she was my brother's teacher- and she was an inspiration. She saw ways to help students who often failed find ways to succeed and even excel. She worked with many of my personal teachers regarding other students- in an era when special education students were pulled out- but her colleagues undoubtedly saw the skill she possessed in moving students forward in learning, and tapped into that- so she visited general education classes with her special education students and helped everyone learn academic skills and life lessons- amazing! It is truly difficult to stop with one (or 2) stories- MANY teachers had a very positive effect on my learning- and my decision to become a teacher, as well.

My seventh grade teacher saw leadership qualities in me. She encouraged me to be involved in student council and the yearbook. It was great to be involved in extracurricular activities with her. She was a teacher, mentor and leader who I looked up to and learned from.

Teacher believed in me and went to great lengths to help me succeed. She would come to school early and help me each and every day.

I had an elementary teacher who took a special interest in me knowing I was going through a tough time at home. She took extra time teaching me to read.

My teacher had creative projects and simulations to involve and get students thinking.

My sixth grade social studies teacher was the BEST teacher! He held students accountable in a caring way. I received my first F on my report card in his class, but he CARED! We happened to move schools together when I was in eighth grade and I was his assistant (he was the AP).

This teacher told us personal and inspiring stories to teach us life lessons. She continually engaged us in conversation and dialogue that had meaning. She had high expectations of us to be good human beings and cared about us beyond only academic excellence.

When the teacher was wrong he admitted it. He taught me about admitting when you are wrong, repairing the relationship and moving forward before restorative practices were "a thing."

My high school math teacher gave me time before school to help me with all of my math classes.

This teacher was always involved and caring. She pushed every student to be their best, and went above and beyond to support and encourage students. She brought many different students together and created a very cohesive group that worked together and supported each other.

He was extremely encouraging and never gave up on his students. He gave up his time before school, at lunch, and after school to ensure his students were successful.

My teacher kept encouraging the class and recognized effort. They acknowledged my reading during Weekly Reader class read-alouds when I fluently read "oceanography" correctly.

I had one sixth grade literature teacher who always smiled and read Shel Silverstein to us. It was a time to be calm, listen, and breathe.

She acted like she cared and took the extra time to help if I did not understand something. She was my third grade teacher.

She was inspiring. She allowed us to develop buddy relationships with younger students. We created our own yearbook that worked on academic skills through meaningful experiences.

I was blessed with many amazing teachers. For me, what sticks out all these years later is that they were there for the kids. They liked kids, they believed they could help us, and they tried to help us. It looked different for everyone. Their relationship with the students made the difference.

My fourth grade teacher made learning fun! Back in 1984 her lessons were engaging and educational!

Since I was a pregnant senior, he refused to give up on me. He made sure I graduated by coming to the house and tutoring me. He brought my work from all my other classes. I graduated a semester early with a high overall GPA. Without him I would have dropped out of high school.

He never gave up, even when I did. He saw more in me than I saw in myself. He had high expectations and always stood up to administration on behalf of his students.

She was always uplifting and positive. She knew I struggled academically but continued to gently push me. Toward the end of the year, she chose to submit one of my writing pieces to our county's writing contest. I did not win the award but still considered myself a winner because she saw my true potential.

My high school history teacher exudes passion for his job, his students and made history come to life.

I struggled academically and three of my high school teachers never gave up on me. They offered help and made such a difference that I chose to be a teacher because of them and their positive influence.

My second grade teacher realized that I was incorrectly placed for reading. (This was the 70s and one you were labeled...) She fought hard to get me reassessed and correctly placed. When that took too long, she just let me go through two reading groups and kept pushing.

(I even took the other level over the summer with my Mom). She kept encouraging my parents too saying that this was too important to give up.

She started a student spotlight and listed our strengths on the door for the whole school to see. The poster featured our pictures and a sample of our work. She did science experiments with us. I remember one on air pressure that failed. She laughed at herself, used it as a teachable moment then tried again. She did activities that encouraged creativity and actively involved our parents/community members.

I was very sick that year (I missed almost 30 days with bronchitis/phenomena). She brought my work to my Mom's work or to the house every week so I wouldn't fall behind. She was the reason I decided to become a teacher.

I came from a very dysfunctional family and the teacher brought me lunch daily. She also went the extra mile to let me stay at her house for Friday/Saturday so that I could participate in the school drama production.

My teacher showed passion with every lesson.

This teacher had very high expectations and rewarded those who met the expectations but never punished those who did not. She had a candy wreath on the classroom door. As the day ended, those who had a good day got to snip a piece of penny candy from the wreath.

She made learning fun.

My fourth grade teacher never gave up on any of her students. She was personable (we knew her first name), creative, and truly cared about all students.

She was my fourth grade teacher and we were her first class. She told us how tall she was, her weight, and invited the entire class to her wedding.

A teacher saw that I was crying and a big mess, from the previous class, and let me take home a final and work on it.

My fifth grade teacher cared so deeply for all her students. She took the time to get to know us as people, not just kids in her class. I waited on her at a restaurant and changed my major back to education the next semester.

My fourth grade teacher had a marble jar we could fill up by staying on task or being good. Marbles would be removed when we were off task and chatty. She only had to swirl the marbles to make us shape up. When the jar was full we got some sort of reward that week. The big prize was a drawing to get to take home her unicycle for the weekend. I can remember getting it twice. (I never mastered it.) I had so many positive teachers in all levels of my education. All the same characteristics, kind, excited about teaching their subject, relatable to students, and visible in our campus life.

My teacher taught with passion and made us work hard, but really cared!

Mrs. O treated us as if we were part of her family. We were all so excited when she told us that she was pregnant.

In elementary school I had a teacher who taught music in our class, which I loved! Then in middle school I had a teacher who had high expectations for learning with quizzes every other day.

My drama teacher made a huge fuss about me moving to her class and made me feel really special!

My first grade teacher always sang songs about how awesome her students were. It made us happy.

My teacher absolutely believed in me and I rose to meet her expectations; I wanted to be who she knew I could be.

She involved me in the classroom and believed I could achieve at high levels. She shared her family with us and made students a part of her life.

My most favorite teacher was my kindergarten teacher. Her soul shined each and every day as she taught us. We all knew she loved us because she told us. She was caring, and never once gave up on anyone in that class, even the friend with the greatest behavior struggles. This teacher will always have a special place in my heart. She was the reason I taught kindergarten for 20 years.

My second grade teacher would read aloud daily and ask us comprehension questions. She also gave everyone a book at the end of the year.

One of my high school classes was really tough, but the teacher never let us quit. He taught and encouraged us until we got it. He offered extra assistance.

My sixth grade teacher believed in me. She constantly encouraged me and made it possible for me to be successful. I became a teacher in large part because of her.

I did not want to write a speech about a research topic because I just did not care. My teacher knew me well enough to find a topic he thought I would be interested in. He pointed me in the right direction and I ended up doing more research than was required because I cared.

My teacher seemed to care about all aspects of my day, or just school.

I just always felt loved.

She is the one that taught me to love learning! She created experiences that allowed us to apply what we knew. She made us responsible for our own learning.

My high school math teachers showed me what learning looked like and how to help kids, even in the teenage years. I appreciated their compassion and hard work. They made me see that learning could be fun and interesting. They really showed me that learning is important.

You knew she was excited to see us every day. She spent a lot of time developing lessons that were meaningful. She expected great things from everyone in the room and would help you when you struggled. She allowed the class to make choices about the output of the assignment. .

All but one of my elementary teachers had a positive effect on me. That one did not have a negative effect, he just left me with minimal memories, neither good nor bad. I had the same teacher for kindergarten and first grade. She was young and excited and loved all the students in our class. She taught me to read. She set an excellent tone for the rest of my school career.

The praise and encouragement that was offered when I needed it most. It was never about what I could not do but what I could do. They believed in a growth mindset before it was even named.

When my father was in the hospital for one of his many stays for his kidney disease, a teacher and his wife took me into their home and watched over me and kept things positive in my life. He was the reason I became a teacher.

My third grade teacher knew all of my six older siblings. She believed in me and always helped me without being angry. She always encouraged me to do my best and told me she saw something in me that she did not see in my other siblings. Too many teachers compared me to them. She did not. She told me I would be an incredible teacher one day. She was right. I think of her often and try to be the person she was to me. I will never forget her and all of the time and energy she put into my success in the classroom.

My teacher said I could do anything, that I was creative and I would be a great role model for students~ that teaching might be my calling.

My first grade teacher is the reason that I became a teacher. She was patient and kind. Kids just gravitated to her. She was always smiling and laughing. She made learning fun and I even would spend my recess walking around talking to her instead of playing.

Mr. Brewer never gave up on us and was always so positive

My teacher always motivated me to be at my best. They were positive, enthusiastic, and energizing. They not only taught the subject, but cared about each student and SMILED.

My elementary teacher was awesome! My middle school teacher took some of us sailing! He played games/connected learning to his own cool games.

I had a female teacher that took notice of a natural skill that I had even when I was not the most popular kid in class.

She was always excited about school and books.

Mrs L is one of the biggest influences on my teaching style. She always did things differently and always faced challenges even when they went wrong.

My teacher connected with me in and OUT of school.

My American Literature teacher gave students choices.

There were many classrooms where I felt like part of a family. We were a team who supported and cared for each other. Those are the years I remember the most.

He could see I was hurting. He told me things would be okay, I just needed to get out of the small town and someone would see and appreciate my beauty.

Everyone still talks about my fourth grade teacher today (decades later) read the entire Little House on the Prairie series to us. She listened and she cared.

My English teacher made me crack up every day. I loved him because of that. It was like he was a stand-up comedian.

My high school English teacher knew I wanted to be a writer, so he went to my grandfather's house to tell him that being a writer was a good thing. When my grandfather asked how he could support me, the teacher told him to get me lots of paper and pencils. For my birthday, I received a stack of lined-paper pads, and boxes of no. 2 pencils. It was the best birthday I ever had.

    My teacher was just a cool person who cared about you.

One of my elementary teachers recognized that I had leadership skills and she appointed me class leader.

He was passionate about history and really loved what he taught.

She saw my interests outside of the classroom and encouraged me in those aspects even though they had nothing to do with her.

My middle school English teacher was encouraging and positive. She taught us the skills so we could be successful. She cared.

My third grade teacher knew life was rough as a kid, she would periodically sneak a light-hearted book into my backpack with a piece of candy just as a way to know she loved me and was thinking of me.

Mrs. S came to school every day prepared and ready. She had a sense of humor and was a consummate professional. She loved high school and could make you feel like the most important person in the room. I did not feel like I found success in school until I took classes with her.

My teacher always reminded me of the greatest and corrected me when I needed it.

My teacher taught me how to write poems and I have never stopped writing.

My third grade teacher always made us all feel like we were the most important children in the world. She has a sign on the door that stated, "Bestest class!"

A teacher that always went above and beyond to make sure I always had what I needed. This includes rides to school, food, social interaction and school work support. She was amazing and an inspiration to me!

I was given extra responsibilities, not just extra work, because I was at the top of my class.

He was excited about the subject matter and made us excited to learn.

This teacher was the definition of above and beyond. It is not easy to create engaging lessons. It takes effort and time but they leave a lasting impression 30 years later.

I had this teacher my last year of high school. It was a very traumatic time in my life as my home life was very tumultuous. This was the yearbook class. I was supposed to have taken Journalism I to begin in Yearbook. However, she made the exception of letting me in the class after requiring me to design a layout, submit a copy, and have an interview with her and the Yearbook committee. That year she gave me all kinds of opportunities to lead, let me run with creative projects, and my idea for the yearbook theme was the one the yearbook staff ended up choosing. She never asked a lot about what was going on at home, but poured into me and encouraged me to persevere and go to college. She also made me see my own potential and believe in myself. Because of her I went to college as a Journalism Major with an emphasis in public relations. What I realized once I was in college is that I did not necessarily love Journalism, I loved what she did for me as a teacher. I changed my major to Elementary Education to impact students like she did me, and counteract the negative experience I had in elementary with my second grade teacher.

My fourth grade teacher had a reading center WAY before anyone else did. It had beanbag chairs, lots of choices, and a rug. He played with us, too. I can remember playing football with him.

The teacher would always teach us about our life and what we needed to learn to be successful, and every kid would always want to be a part of that class.

My band instructor was dedicated and caring, yet very strict. He expected much from his students, which made us want to perform to the absolute best of our abilities. We didn't want to disappoint someone who was so wonderful to us.

My teachers would care. They would help me care for me, I could talk to them and look up to them. But now that we are older teachers expect us to know and do everything.

I had messed up and she was there to comfort me, let me eat lunch in her room even if other teachers were there and give me ideas to help/solve the situation. She was overall an amazing teacher and always looked out for her students.

We sang songs, made creative projects, read stories, laughed, did science experiments, went outside, laughed, wrote and shared our stories, participated in simulations, laughed and enjoyed learning.

My first grade teacher was all business from the second you walked in. She had a job to do and by golly she was going to achieve it with all of her kids. What made her stick out besides her work ethic, was at the end of the year they realigned the school district and were sending me across town to a different elementary school. She tried to convince administration it was not what was best for the kids, but had no luck, so in July on her summer vacation, called my parents directly, walked them through her worries and what I would need. I was no longer her student, but I would always be one of her "kids".

Mr. D thought I was smart!

In sixth grade, my teacher told me that he believed in me, and in my potential for long term academic success. He was the first teacher to believe in my abilities, and because of that, taught me how to believe in myself. His expectations were high, but he taught me the value of hard work and engendered a hunger for knowledge in me. I learned extremely advanced topics in that class (political systems and processes, ancient communications and languages, early literature, military history, and much more). I will graduate next year with my PhD, in large part because of him.

My fourth grade teacher worked with me and gave me the confidence that I could do better.

My AP English teacher read every book on the New York Times, "Best Seller" list for 20 years. He made us write. He taught us to write on demand. He was brilliant. He read to us, using voices for characters...sadly by the time I went back to thank him, he had passed away. He is the reason I became an English teacher.

There are so many more positive teachers than negative! I still remember a high school teacher encouraging me to do early acceptance to college because she knew I was the best candidate (her words). Teachers who were involved in my extracurricular activities were the best!

My high school history teacher dressed up as a WWII soldier and acted out a scene from a book we were reading getting everyone involved spontaneously.

Mr. K. was an art teacher who somehow got himself locked in a closet. I was, in part, one of the students who saved him.

My third grade teacher was AMAZING..... she truly let you know she cared about you and was always there to help. She took time to check in on kids when they were absent from school while they were sick. She made time to be outside on recess even when she was not on duty. She also was creative, and really loved her job. As a result, her students LOVED her class.

My teacher let me take breaks in her room and just was there for me 24/7.

She would talk to me about non-school related things and would still help me with things I did not understand.

My high school teacher taught me that every answer can be right if you have proof and that truth is not always the same as fact. In order to demonstrate this, we drew our hand- the physical aspects of our hands. Then on the other side he had us draw our truth- how we felt about our hands then compare how we were thinking during the exercise.

She always made me feel I was loved and cared about as a person. I had her as a teacher 49 years ago and we still are in touch, getting together about every six months to a year for dinner. I am now a teacher and she gives me great teaching advice.

She did a read-aloud story for 15 minutes per day, just after lunch. She was so kind. She even had a class party at her home. She was so nice to everyone!

I had a social studies teacher who was also a football coach. He loved history and made it come alive. He was always supportive and encouraging to all students.

I had two English teachers in high school who loved what they did, and their enthusiasm was infectious. They both made me feel smart and capable every day. I ended up getting an undergraduate degree in English Literature and later a Master's in Education because of those teachers.

References

Amir, O. and Biederman, I. (November, 2016). The Neural Correlates of Humor Creativity. Retrieved from: https://internal-journal.frontiersin.org/articles/10.3389/fnhum.2016.00597/full

Ayllón, S., Alsina, A., & Colomer, J. (May 24, 2019). Teachers' Involvement andStudents' Self-efficacy: Keys to Achievement in Higher Education. Retrieved from: https://journals.plos.org/plosone/article?id=10.1371/journal.pone.0216865

Association of Curriculum Development and Supervision (ASCD). (2014). Teacher Leadership: The What, Why, and How of Teachers as Leaders. Retrieved from: *https://www.ascd.org/ASCD/pdf/siteASCD/wholechild/fall2014wcsreport.pdf*

Bergland, C. (2015). The Neuroscience of Recalling Old Memories. *PsychologyToday*. Retrieved from: https://www.psychologytoday.com/us/blog/the-athletes-way/201507/the-neuroscience-recalling-old-memories

Boston, M. (February, 2017). How Being Funny Changes Your Brain. Retrieved from: https://news.usc.edu/116675/studying-creativity-and-the-brain-is-no-joke/

Burns, M. (February, 2019). I'm a Neuroscientist. Here's How Teachers Change Kids' Brains. Retrieved from: https://www.edsurge.com/news/2019-02-19-i-m-a-neuroscientist-here-s-how-teachers-change-kids-brains

Dean, N. (April 10, 2020). Unlocking the Wisdom of the Brain. Retrieved from: https://brainworldmagazine.com/unlocking-wisdom-brain/

Gohd, C. (2020). We May Have Just Figured Out How the Brain Processes Good and Bad Experiences. Neoscope. Retrieved from: https://futurism.com/neoscope/may-have-figured-out-how-brain-processes-good-bad-experiences

Edwards, S. (2010). Humor, Laughter, and Those Aha Moments. Retrieved from: https://hms.harvard.edu/news/humor-laughter-those-aha-moments

Kath. (2017). 10 Wise and Beautiful Quotes from Maya Angalu. Retrieved from:https://forreadingaddicts.co.uk/authors/10-wise-beautiful-quotes-maya-angelou/

Kraut, R. (2017). Stanford Encyclopedia of Philosophy. Retrieved from: https://plato.stanford.edu/entries/plato/

LaGravenese, R. (Director). (2007). Freedom Writers. [Film]. MTV and Jersey Films.

Lynch, M. (November 17, 2015). Five Professional Commitments You Need to Make as a Teacher. Retrieved from: https://www.theedadvocate.org/5-professional-commitments-you-need-to-make-as-a-teacher/

Mackenzie, S., Morrell, B.J.,& Cook, S. (August, 2004). A View From the Inside: Continuing the Conversation About Teaching in Maine. Augusta, Maine; Maine Education Leadership Consortium.

Meeks, T. & Jeste, D. (2009). Neurobiology of Wisdom?: Literature Overview. Retrieved from: https://www.ncbi.nlm.nih.gov/pmc/articles/PMC3698847/

Metter, A.(Director). (1986). Back to School. [Film]. Paper Clip Productions.

Raypole, C. (September, 2019). How to Hack Your Hormones for a Better Mood. Retrieved from: *https://www.healthline.com/health/happy-hormone*

Rossen, E. (January, 2021). Preventing School from Becoming the 11th ACE. Keynote presentation at the Maine Principals' Association.

Shanker, S. (n.d.) "Reframing" Challenging Behaviour, Part 1: Blue Brain, Red Brain, and Brown Brain. Retrieved from: https://self-reg.ca/reframing-challenging-behaviour-part-1/

Siegle, S. (May, 2020). The Art of Kindness - Mayo Clinic Health System. Retrieved from: https://www.mayoclinichealthsystem.org/hometown-health/speaking-of-health/the-art-of-kindness

Souers, K. & Hall, P. (2020, October). Trauma is a Word, Not a Sentence. Retrieved from: https://www.ascd.org/el/articles/trauma-is-a-word-not-a-sentence

Sparks, S. (March 12, 2019). Why Teacher-Student Relationships Matter. Retrieved from: https://www.edweek.org/teaching-learning/why-teacher-student-relationships-matter/2019/03

Sprenger, M. (2020). Social-Emotional Learning and the Brain: Strategies to Help Your Students Learn. ASCD. Retrieved from: https://www.google.com/books/edition/Social_Emotional_Learning_and_the_Brain/6KT8DwAAQBAJ?hl=en&gbpv=1&dq=inauthor:%22Marilee+Sprenger%22&printsec=frontcover

Starr, L. (2003). Are You A Bully? Retrieved from: http://www.educationworld.com/a_curr/columnists/starr_points/starr027.shtml

Trafton, A. (2015, April). How the Brain Tells Good from Bad. Brain and Cognitive Sciences. Retrieved from: https://bcs.mit.edu/news-events/news/how-brain-tells-good-bad

Vandergriendt, C. (Jul, 2020). What's the Difference Between Dopamine and Serotonin? Retrieved from: https://www.healthline.com/health/dopamine-vs-serotonin

Ward, T. (January 13, 2017). Wisdom of the Brain: 5 Questions on Neuroscience and the Helping Professions for Dr. Cameron J. Thomas. Retrieved from: https://www.huffpost.com/entry/wisdom-of-the-brain-5-que_b_14140726

Watson Caring Science Institute. (2021). Caring Science & Human Caring Theory. Retrieved from: https://www.watsoncaringscience.org/jean-bio/caring-science-theory/

Wentzel, G. & Ramani, G. (2016). Handbook of Social Influences in School Contexts: Social-Emotional, Motivation, and Cognitive Outcomes. Routledge.

Wong, H. K. (2002). Induction: The Best Form of Professional Development. Retrieved from: http://www.ascd.org/publications/educational-leadership/mar02/vol59/num06/Induction@-The-Best-Form-of-Professional-Development.aspx

About the Authors

Dr. Holly Blair is the Executive Director of the Maine Principals' Association Professional Division in Augusta, Maine. She is in charge of providing high quality professional development for educational leaders throughout the state of Maine. She is also a college professor, author, and speaker. She works with educators and presenters from all over the United States. She has served as a classroom teacher, a teaching principal, and a principal in several school districts. Follow her on Twitter @HollyBlairMPA.

Dr. Rick Jetter is the Assistant Head of Schools at the Western NY Maritime Charter School in Buffalo, NY. He is the author of nine other books for educators and is a well-known national speaker and presenter. He is also the co-founder of Pushing Boundaries Consulting, LLC. You can find out more about Rick at www.rickjetter.com and on most social media channels at @RickJetter.

Bring "You Are #1" to Your School or Organization

Follow the hashtag: **#YouAreNumber1** and invite Holly and Rick to your next event! They can provide in-person or virtual training for your school or organization on the ideas brought forth in this book, along with other topics related to:

- School leadership
- Student motivation
- Creating a positive culture and climate
- Innovative leadership
- Powerful research-based instructional strategies
- SEL in the classroom
- Equity and equality for a NEW era of schooling

And much, much more!

Through their vibrant and hilarious story-telling and depth of experience and knowledge in the field of education for a combined total of over 50 years, Holly and Rick first met at a national conference. Because of this, Holly invited Rick and his co-author Rebecca Coda to present two of their books at the Maine Principals' Annual Spring Conference in 2019.

From there, they hit it off and became great friends who decided to work on this FIRST EVER project in education--an idea never conceived or developed by anyone ever before!